TRIVBITS #1

Amusing and Amazing Stories and Trivia Tidbits

JIM WILLARD

MJW PUBLISHING COMPANY

TRIVBITS #1: Amusing and Amazing Stories and Trivia Tidbits

Published by
MJW Publishing Company
PO Box 3074
Loveland, Colorado 80539 USA

First Edition 2005

9 8 7 6 5 4 3 2 1

ISBN 0-9762586-0-9

*To those whose minds
occasionally wander
and then find themselves
on familiar paths.*

They Weren't Radio Dinners

I may be stepping into dangerous territory here but since they've never been a staple (I did get one of those in a homemade pizza once) of my diet I feel comfortable in addressing TV dinners.

Frozen pot pies came into being in 1951 but in 1954 the Swanson Foods Company of Omaha broke culinary ground, figuratively, with the TV dinner. The entire dinner came in an aluminum tray so no mixing, slicing or mashing was required; no dishwashing or plates got in the way.

Swanson called its product a TV dinner not so much because you ate in front of the set but in that era TV symbolized the modern day. The first versions even came in a box that was designed to resemble a television console.

The first TV dinner was, guess what, turkey? The sophistication of these taste delights progressed to Hungry Man and Lean Cuisine and then to Le Menu in the 1980s with its list of suggested accompanying wines (I can't believe it!). My guess is that the little rascals will outlive me as an element of our culture, but since I don't eat them I've got that on my side.

• Mark Twain's advice may be pertinent here. "Part of the secret of success in life is to eat what you like and let the food fight it out inside."

• It didn't surprise me in the least. John Wayne played more leading roles than any other actor in movie history. The Duke appeared in 153 movies playing the lead in 142. His career began with *The Drop Kick* in 1927 and closed out with *The Shootist* in 1976.

• Keeping score at Christmas? If your loved ones gave you all the gifts mentioned in "The Twelve Days of Christmas" you'd have 364 items and probably a really messy house.

• The date was "post-Tea Party." The Duchess of Bedford instituted the British custom of formal afternoon tea about 1840. Crumpets were probably served along with those ghastly little cucumber sandwiches.

• Go ahead and finish this column. If you are a man aged 60 or over the odds of you dying in the next three hours are about one in 150,000.

• Do you really think horses care? That custom of mounting a horse from the left stems from medieval days when most knights had a sword and scabbard on their left side for an easy right-hand draw thus making a mount with the right leg going over the horse's back much easier.

Even though cowboys like Gene and Roy bounded onto Champion and Trigger from the back most of us mount the occasional horse from the left because "that's the way it's done." Horses are trained to expect the left mount but what if you trained in the opposite?

❧ Fort Fizzle wasn't a post you'd want on your resumé if you were a soldier in the late 1800s. The fort was established in the Bitterroot Valley of Montana to stop the Nez Perce Indians on their retreat from the Wallowa Valley in Oregon. Chief Joseph and his followers simply went around the fort and proceeded on their way.

❧ The first Pocket Book published nationally in the U.S. was James Hilton's *Lost Horizon* in 1939. Felix Salten's *Bambi* was also published that year. Both led to fine movies although Hilton's title was changed to *Lost Horizons*.

❧ This Hebrew proverb offers hope for some of us. "Whoever has not tasted sinfulness does not qualify for holiness." If you haven't tasted I wouldn't go right out and act on this.

❧ Some early culture had a lot of time on its figurative hands. There are 838 stone monoliths on Easter Island.

❧ Beware wandering about in the Bahamas during a "banana wind." The wind isn't strong enough to peel them, but it's just enough below hurricane velocity to blow the fruit off the trees.

An Un-uniform Uniform?

In many ways, they are a type of uniform and some are large enough to double as multi-colored tents. The garment under discussion is the Hawaiian shirt. I've just had the opportunity to view a number of them firsthand.

The origin of the shirt dates from the arrival of missionaries on the Hawaiian Islands and the insistence that the naked islanders put on some clothes. The shirts and muumuus were sized large and loose and dyed with native dyes that faded over washes.

It wasn't until 1924 (and Dupont's introduction of rayon) that the shirts as we know them were somewhat standardized. GI's returning from the World War II Pacific operations stopped off in

Honolulu and bought the "go-to-hell" shirts as souvenirs.

Montgomery Ward's catalog of 1952 even offered an array of the gaudy shirts for vacationers to the tropics. I—like many of my male readers—have one that I drag out for special occasions and the beauty of the shirt is that it never seems to go out of style. In addition, the size seems to accommodate my dietary excursions.

🐾 Here's another one of those great "How many dogs does it take to change a light bulb?" responses from an Australian shepherd. "First, I'll put the light bulbs in a little circle, then …"

🐾 I haven't the foggiest idea why he'd ever need a horse but the name of Superman's horse was Comet.

🐾 For many people it's the worst possible thing they could ever have to do. They're afflicted with glossophobia, poor souls. Glossophobia is the fear of speaking in public.

Do your kids and grandkids a favor (mine have almost forgiven me); get them up in public as soon as you can. They'll never become glossophobics.

🐾 Grandfather clocks weren't simply a generation older than father clocks. The first weight-and-pendulum clock was developed by a Dutch scientist, Christian Huygens, in the 1650s. The clocks became known as long-case clocks and were status symbols in German-settled Pennsylvania. Henry Clay Work, an American songwriter, referred to long-case clocks in a song he wrote in 1876 "My Grandfather's Clock" and the name stuck.

❖ Red light, turn right, driver's delight. A right-turn on red—after a complete stop—is permitted in all states where not otherwise prohibited by a sign. New York City is the only major city prohibiting the act. Actually, a right-turn on red saves each driver 14 seconds at a turn, cuts gasoline and exhaust emissions and facilitates more traffic at intersections. On top of that, the Federal Highway Administration states that fewer accidents occur during right turns on red than during right turns on green. One good turn deserves another.

❖ Here's a Mexican proverb some of us have learned the hard way: "Wounds from the knife are healed, but not those from the tongue."

❖ The most popular musical group in the world in 1977 had a palindrome as a name. ABBA was made up of Agatha, Bjorn, Benny and Annafrid, two couples with the last names of Ulvaeus and Andersson. Interestingly enough they could also have made a palindrome of their last names UAAU or AUUA but ABBA was the choice and the group was the largest grossing export in Sweden in 1978 beating out Volvo. My Volvo does get better gas mileage than their records.

❖ When you stop to think about it (remember to start again) inventing a word that enters common usage is quite a trick. William Shakespeare's invention of more than 1,700 words in his career puts him a few more than 1,700 ahead of me.

It All Began With …

🐚 Many of us owe our excellent start in education to Friedrich Froebel. No, he wasn't my kindergarten teacher (that was Miss Cline), but he did develop the first kindergarten in 1837, a few years prior to my enrollment. Friedrich had suffered an unhappy childhood which engendered in him a love of children so he set up his Child Nurturing and Activity Institute in Blankenburg, Germany.

The inspiration for the name kindergarten came during a walk in the woods. A "child's garden" should be a place where children "are cultivated in accordance with the laws of their own being, of God and of Nature." Froebel's concept made sense to a number of educators, and kindergartens flourished as a vehicle to introduce children to learning in a friendly, loving way. Kindergartens are fun to visit.

The little inmates are still innocent and love to have stories told to them.

The Spanish Main wasn't the major throughway in Madrid. The term was the former name of the Caribbean Sea as the main route of Spanish treasure galleons.

One of their team jerseys would be worth a lot of money today. A manpower shortage during World War II led to an NFL team being formed with members from both the Pittsburgh Steelers and the Philadelphia Eagles. Naturally, they called it the Steagles.

Try this one on a summer night, "Say, doesn't that sound like stridulation?" Stridulation is the technical word for the sound made by crickets (or other critters) by rubbing together parts of the body. I suppose technically it applies to humans, but I wouldn't want to be around.

Seeing the first fifty-star flag unfurled must have been a real treat. If you were at Fort McHenry, Maryland in 1960 you'd have seen it waving in the spot where Francis Scott Key saw it in the light of the "rocket's red glare."

I wonder how they'd feel about an Adam and Eve float. Humboldt, Kansas hosts an annual "Biblesta"—a combination of Bible and fiesta—parade every year where all the people on floats must wear biblical costumes.

It just makes you want to brush your teeth! Milton Bradley marketed its game Candyland as a "Sweet Little Game for Sweet Little Folks."

❦ Many of us are in tune with J.B. Priestly who said, "When I was young there was no respect for the young, and now that I am old, there is no respect for the old. I missed out coming and going."

❦ Yuckkk!! A giraffe can clean out its ears using its tongue. Don't try this at home. I decline any responsibility either fiscal or moral.

❦ Really bored? Both Custer, South Dakota and Vail, Arizona are homes to replicas of Bedrock Village where the Flintstones lived.

❦ Let's hear it for the Vets. Twenty-two of the forty-three U.S. presidents served in the military.

❦ Do you believe in the "philosopher's stone"? In medieval times, alchemists believed that the powers of the stone would turn base metals into gold. The quest for the stone was the stimulus for the science that became our modern chemistry.

❦ "I passed my electrocardiogram," said Tom wholeheartedly.

❦ Not tonight, dear, I have a nosebleed. Attila the Hun succumbed to a nosebleed and died on his wedding night in 453 A.D. No information exists as to whether the gifts from Hun guests were returned.

You Are What You Eat?

🐾 Interested in food and aren't we all? We cultivate only about one hundred of the 500,000 known plant species. Of that hundred, thirty provide us with 85 percent of our food and 95 percent of our calories and protein.

Three-fourths of our food comes from eight crops in the cereal categories (no, not Sugar-Frosted Flakes). Those super eight are rice, wheat, oats, barley, corn, millet, rye and sorghum. And we really only chomp sixteen of the 4,500 mammal species.

There's good stuff out there like Buffalo gourd, a desert melon loaded with starch and proteins and Prairie potato once grown by the Plains Indians with protein content three times that of a conventional

potato. It's just a matter of changing our taste preferences.

🐾 I just ran onto this series of light bulb jokes. How many Border Collies does it take to change a light bulb? Just one, when he's done he'll replace any other wiring not up to code. Or how many Malamutes does it take to change a light bulb? He'll say, "Let the Border Collie do it. You can feed me while he's busy." Twoey would simply watch and applaud both.

🐾 Take your own survey if you like but prior surveys indicate American men prefer boxers to briefs by a two-to-one margin. I try to treat subjects like this delicately.

🐾 Want to get the most mileage out of a day of vacation? Take Tuesday off. Tuesday is the most productive day of the five-day workweek. I could never make that recommendation when I was a manager in Personnel.

🐾 They may still be watching, but I swear they didn't make me write this. Project Sign was the name of the Air Force's first study of UFO's which began in 1947. The name of the study was changed to Project Grudge—I wouldn't want to aggravate them—in 1949 and then in 1951 to Project Blue Book. The UFO investigations were terminated in 1969 (only to be picked up by "The X Files").

🐾 The "Saturday Night Massacre" sounds like something right out of the Wild West. Well, not exactly, it was right out of the "Wild West Wing."

The name was given to the night of October 20, 1973 when President Nixon ordered Attorney General Eliot Richardson to fire the Watergate Special Prosecutor Archibald Cox. Richardson refused and resigned in protest. Nixon then ordered the Deputy A. G. William Ruckelshaus to fire Cox. Ruckelshaus refused and was fired. Nixon then named U.S. Solicitor Robert Bork (rhymes with Dork) the executor and he fired Cox. Final score: Honorable Men 3, Nixon 0.

❧ Let's have a moment of honored silence for Ruth G. Wakefield. She invented the chocolate chip cookie in 1930.

❧ I guess he knew where the butter was on his bread. Jerome Kern published only one song in his great career that was not written specifically for a stage musical or a motion picture. That song was "The Last Time I Saw Paris," which ironically became the title of a non-musical movie made in 1954, nine years after Kern's death.

❧ Occasionally we see those referred to in this Hebrew proverb. "The worst kind of person is one whose power of speech is greater than his power of thought."

❧ Alaska not only sports the highest mountain in the U.S. it also contains the next four in altitude. Foraker at 17,400 feet is near Mt. McKinley, but St. Elias, Bona and Blackburn at 18,008, 16,550 and 16,390 respectively are in the very lower southeast part of the state. Why, because they're there.

❧ Wild rice isn't really. That is, it isn't rice. It's a coarse, annual grass that flourishes in shallow marshes and streams. You can pick your own in Minnesota if you choose to challenge the mosquitoes for it.

Buddy, Watch Your Step

❧ The difference between theirs and ours almost got me in England a few years ago. As I went to cross a street in London I looked to my left for oncoming traffic and seeing none started to step into the street only to hear a horn from my right.

We consider residents of the United Kingdom, Ireland, India, Australia, South Africa, Indonesia and a few others to be driving on the wrong side of the road. They feel the same way about us. How did it all get started?

The left-side proponents cite a time when parties passing in a narrow road moved left to allow a free "sword-hand"— their right—and the left on the reins of the horse. This held true until 1300 AD when Pope Boniface VIII who believed "all

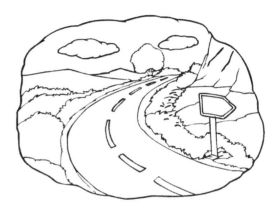

roads led to Rome" insisted pilgrims travel in on the left side.

That worked for 500 years or until the French Revolution when the rebels insisted no pope was going to dictate their traffic rules. This move to the right was institutionalized by Napoleon in France and all the other countries he conquered.

The U.S. adopted the French approach

not to spite the British but because early wagons had no seat and the driver sat on the left-rear horse. To ensure a safe pass of two wagons one had to observe the left side wheel hubs.

Finally in 1792 Pennsylvania passed the first legislation requiring driving on the right-hand side of the road. Other states followed suit and early autos had the driver's seat on the left side of the car. The Brits and related countries chose not to change. Look both ways before crossing.

🖎 Perhaps some of you name your useful family tools. I've never had occasion to do that. Carry Nation, the well-known temperance activist, name the three hatchets she used to destroy saloons Faith, Hope and Charity.

🖎 Do-it-yourselfers could certainly give him a chorus of "For he's a jolly good Fellows." Alvin J. Fellows invented the tape measure. He received a patent for it in 1868.

🖎 Having seen him, it's difficult to understand why the crooner of the 1930–40s, Rudy Vallee, was nicknamed "The Vagabond Lover."

🖎 Bob Phillips cautioned, "Two things never live up to their advertising claims: the circus and sin." He's probably right. The last circus I saw was disappointing.

🖎 In the lifetime of an average American, that person will borrow 374 different items (books, tapes, videos, etc.) from a library. No data is available on how many are returned.

❦ "D4D" was the name first used for the U.S. Army's canine force. "Dogs For Defense" was quickly superseded by K-9 Corps as World War II GI's created their own language of abbreviations.

❦ The first "minimum wage" established by the U.S. Congress occurred in 1938. The amount was 25 cents per hour. It took an hour to "get in your two-bits worth."

❦ For a few years it was quite a popular style. That funny looking two-cornered hat Napoleon wore is called a "bicorn." The early American colonists wore "tricorns." I had one in college that I made with homecoming pins. My dog ultimately ate it.

❦ The meaning isn't how it sounds or is spelled. Sitomania is not the urge to become a couch potato. Sitomania is an abnormal craving for food (which could even include broccoli).

❦ Kraft Laboratory technicians invented Cheez Whiz in 1951 (deliberately). They were searching for a product that wouldn't get lumpy or oily when heated like real cheese. Housewives found 1,304 uses for it in testmarketing. You don't want to know some of the uses.

❦ The connection isn't immediately obvious. The theme song of James Cagney's gangster classic *Public Enemy* was "I'm Forever Blowing Bubbles."

A Pinch of This, A Dab of That?

Maybe you've seen the little sign in a friend's kitchen, "Kissin' don't last, cookin' do." I don't have any evidence as to the first part of that premise but I can testify to the second half. Even though thousands of families eat out frequently still other thousands join the cooking fraternity/sorority every year.

All three of my kids are gourmet cooks, but if not for Fannie Farmer they (and their mom) might still be struggling. Why Fannie? She wrote *The Boston Cooking School Cookbook* in 1896. The tome was the first to standardize measurements and then have the foods kitchen-tested. She encouraged level measurements and time and temperature directions. By 1959, her

publisher had sold more than three million copies of her work. The most popular cookbooks of all time are *The Better Homes & Gardens New Cookbook* (a relative newcomer in 1930) and *The Joy of Cooking* published the next year. So, thanks Fannie, and *bon appetit*.

🐾 Robots (not the science fiction type) are prevalent in American industry today, but do you know where the word originated? Samuel Butler first used the word "robot" in his 1872 novel *Erewhon* (nowhere spelled backwards).

🐾 Is there a strange connection here? Green was the color of Mr. Spock's blood on "Star Trek" and the color of the Thing's blood in the 1951 movie. Green was the color of the *Streetcar Named Desire* and the color of the dress Scarlett O'Hara made from the drapes at Tara. You tell me. Is this an "X Files" issue?

🐾 The Pianola is not a small mobile piano. The Pianola is a small statue awarded annually to lyric writers and composers selected for the Songwriter's Hall of Fame (based on hit songs written).

🐾 I'm not much of a poker player. I don't know when to hold 'em, but I do know when to fold 'em. If I drew the ace of diamonds, ace of clubs, eight of spades, eight of clubs and queen of hearts I'd pitch 'em quick. Many will remember that as the "Dead Man's Hand" held by James Butler (Wild Bill) Hickok on August 2, 1876 in Deadwood, South Dakota. Jack McCall shot James—I didn't know him well enough to call him by his nickname—in Saloon #10 or one of several other saloons all claiming to be where he was shot. Perhaps McCall shot him then dragged the body around town. It's a good story and probably mostly true.

🐾 Keep a good grip on yours. Nearly half of the Americans who responded to a poll said they would donate the organs of deceased relatives without first securing their permission.

❧ The juices most consumed in the United States are in order: orange, apple, blends, grape and grapefruit. Prune tapped in at sixth with some senior votes.

❧ Pan American served the first hot airline meals on one of their flights in 1935. Some of those same meals may be available today.

❧ I offer another topical country-western song title, "While I Was Out Jogging, She Was Running Around."

❧ That structure we call the Quonset Hut came about its name directly. The huts were first manufactured in Quonset, Rhode Island during World War II. For a number of years after the war, the huts made up married student housing at South Dakota State College. It must have made the veterans feel right at home.

❧ Picture this if you dare. Dolly Parton played the snare drum in her high school marching band.

❧ Contrary to some folks' opinions of their relatives or in-laws, there has never been a monkey native to the United States.

❧ The names Siger and Violet Holmes don't spark any particular memories, but maybe you knew their offspring Sherlock and Mycroft. Arthur Conan Doyle gave his famous detective a heritage.

Books For Eternity

I've noticed a number of book clubs recently, Oprah's among them. So, I've decided to start Jim's Book Club. No, the books won't be trivia books. I've decided to avoid competition with current book clubs over the latest releases and to focus on exceptional books from the past you may have overlooked. I've also decided to schedule my reviews on a random basis to allow myself flexibility in searching out these "quaint and curious" tomes "of forgotten lore." We'll see how it goes.

Jim's Book Club—Review Number One. The title is *Blooming: A Small-Town Girlhood.* Well, first you're asking, "Why did he read this?" My response is because it's a good book and one can never learn enough about the opposite (I mean that kindly) gender.

Susan Allen Toth has told an endearing story of growing up in a small midwestern town (Ames, Iowa) in the 1950s. The story is at turns, funny, poignant, wise and charming. She captures her examples of many of my memories and presents a lifestyle and community we've almost forgotten. The book is more than 20 years old but may still be found in your local used book store or by special order through them. It's worth the read and would be a nice reminder to a daughter or granddaughter of "the way we were."

❧ Now that we're in a somewhat literary vein, here's a Tom Swifty for you. "'I'll have to take the telegrapher's test again,' said Tom remorsefully."

❧ You might ask where do they go since we don't fill skyscrapers with them. Each year, we Americans use enough foam packaging peanuts to fill twenty 85-story skyscrapers. And no, even with a good dip your guests won't like them.

❧ At their size you wouldn't think they'd need the gang concept for protection. Lions are the only cats that like group (pride) living.

❧ "All day I face the barren waste without the taste of water." Our planet is turning to desert at the pace of about 40 square miles in every 24 hours.

❧ Steven Wright is a funny guy. He offers this comment that may have come from a high school reunion. "I like to reminisce with people I don't know. Granted it takes longer."

❧ Ever see a "gustnado"? It's a small dusty tornado that precedes a bigger tornado. The trick is getting out of there just before the transition.

❧ I was a math major but never memorized this formula, "the area of a square is measured by his height, weight and suit size."

❧ I don't know about you but when a recipe calls for zest in the flavoring I check out the soap supply. Imagine my surprise to discover zest is the outermost part of the rind of a lemon or an orange. To correctly remove this one needs a special tool called a zester, just another ploy to sell unique kitchen implements.

❧ Rabbits live in warrens and badgers live in setts (I didn't know that) while Mongolian nomads live in yurts. To each his own, I'll take my comfortable patio home where the only undomesticated creatures are the grandchildren.

❧ The award probably isn't presented every year like it was a few years ago, but its winners still live in my memories based on my Saturday afternoon acquaintanceships. The Silver Spur Award was given annually to the best actor in a western movie.

❧ The date, 1924, marked a passage in history. That year was the last time Sears Catalogue carried an advertisement for "White Duck Emigrant Wagon Covers."

❧ Those little lights last a long time. In an average day an American opens the refrigerator 22 times.

His Music Blended With the Times

❧ Was this guy both a musical chart topper and an electro-mechanical wizard? I'll give him credit for the first, but we must recognize Fred Osius for the second. Fred Waring and his Pennsylvanians had more than fifty recordings hit pop charts from 1923 to 1954, and his radio shows were extremely popular during the '30s and '40s so we can give him credit for that.

The other Fred (Osius) was actually the inventor of the blender that became the "Waring Blendor." The second Fred was the brother-in-law of the first Fred's publicity director. He (Osius) invented and patented a blender in the 1930s, but he didn't know how to develop the marketing and promotion needed to generate sales. So, the second Fred convinced the first Fred to start a company and to take the blender on the road with his band tour in 1938.

Waring named the company (and the product) after himself and used it to mix drinks in bars along the way. The demonstrations were a big success. Sales picked up and by 1947 the Waring Blendor was available for home purchase and use. The moral of the story is you can't tell your Fred's without a scorecard. Oh, by the way, the second Fred called his invention "The Miracle Mixer."

♬ The scientific name is "Geococcyx californianus" (easy for me to type, *not*). You'd know it as the Roadrunner. In reality, it doesn't go "Beep, beep" but it does move along sprightly. The late Mel Blanc used to do the beeps. The bird is actually a member of the cuckoo family, which may explain some of the behaviors.

♬ The Roy Rogers Museum in Branson, Missouri has many of the late actor's artifacts. Trigger—Roy's horse, Buttermilk—Dale's horse, and Bullet—Roy's dog, are all stuffed and on display in the museum. Don't ask, Roy was buried elsewhere.

♬ The faculty could have included the brilliant Galileo. Harvard University was founded in 1636, five years prior to Galileo's death. John Harvard, a New Towne (now Cambridge, Massachusetts) clergyman was its first benefactor. He donated 300 books and 800 English pounds to get things rolling.

The school was named after him in 1638 and has graduated more U.S. presidents than any other college. I don't suppose I could start Willard University by donating 300 trivia books and a couple of grand today.

♬ Keep this in mind if you want. One good thing about apathy is that you don't have to exert yourself to show you're sincere in your belief.

♬ It's no wonder you don't hear songbirds whistling "Take me home, country roads." There are more than 380 publicly-funded wildlife refuges in the United

States. The refuges are home to 220-plus species of animals, 600-plus kinds of birds and thousands of plants, fish, amphibians, etc. West Virginia has no wildlife refuges; it's the only state without.

👉 Lose an occasional golf ball? Try this tip from Michael Miles for finding a ball in the rough. "First look ten yards past where you think you hit it out, then look ten yards short, and finally look five yards further into the rough." If that fails, estimate where it should have gone and play from there.

👉 In a related palindrome, "Golf? No, sir, prefer prison flog."

👉 Not that it matters unless you're on that side, but bats always turn left when they're leaving a cave.

👉 How Hester Won Her "A." Each year more than 5 million copies of the Cliff notes for *The Scarlet Letter* are sold in America.

👉 I certainly wouldn't have considered it a complimentary nickname myself, and maybe he didn't either. Singer ("I'm Calling You ooooo..") Nelson Eddy was known as "The Singing Capon."

👉 Just read that there are so many foreign cars in Beverly Hills that it has been two years since any pedestrians were hit above the knees.

It's Not Chicken Feed

❧ My little friends come right up to the railing on my deck to say thanks for a great meal. No, I'm not talking about an exquisite dinner party although that would be fun, too.

We have a restricted access (no Grackles, blackbirds, starlings, crows or condors) bird feeder on the edge of some wetlands behind us.

Most of the birds we attract are finches, but that shouldn't be surprising. One of every seven birds in the world is a finch. Finches seem to like this delicate combination of mixed seeds we purchase for them, but I do question how they got by without our help in ages past, especially if more than 14 percent of all the world's birds are finches.

I wonder if this isn't a conspiracy and the finches have major holdings in the bird seed industry that has sprung up in the last few years. Conspiracies seem to be everywhere. Next they'll fly in for lunch in black helicopters.

❧ By the way, next time you wish on a furcula keep this in mind. The scientific name for a bird's (turkeys included) wishbone is a furcula.

❧ I usually try to avoid items that might be particularly sensitive to some readers, but I felt compelled to mention that Joseph C. Gayetty invented the first packaged bathroom tissue in 1857.

❧ The play itself didn't make a huge splash when it opened on Broadway in October of 1930, but the orchestra was noteworthy. "Girl Crazy" by George and Ira Gershwin had in its first-night orchestra: Jimmy Dorsey, Benny Goodman, Gene Krupa, Glenn Miller and Jack Teagarden. Red Nichols was the leader. That group yielded six incredible bands and hundreds of hit records.

❧ "Westward-ho!" has the ring of a term spawned by the westward expansion of the United States. *Au contrere* (French for "to the contrary," just an educational insight) was coined by William Shakespeare in "Twelfth Night."

❧ If you're taking sildenafil citrate, don't worry. Your secret is safe with me (it may not be with Bob Dole). I won't tell anyone—else—that it is the chemical name for Viagra.

❧ Would you watch a TV action show titled "Skill"? Probably not, but thousands watched "Kung Fu" at its peak of popularity and *kung fu* is Chinese for "skill."

❧ Did you know that for a brief period (1795–1818) the U.S. flag had fifteen stars and fifteen stripes? In 1818 Congress decided to return the stripes to the number of original colonies and increase just the stars with additional states.

❧ As I ready myself for a well-deserved nap I reflect on the fact that the typical American will spend 24 years sleeping in his or her lifetime, and I may be slightly behind the appropriate pace.

❧ Next time I may bring my own container and cut the cost. The most expensive component in a bucket of buttered movie popcorn is the bucket. It costs about five times as much as the popcorn, and the "butter" is artificial which costs only one tenth of the container. All that said I still have difficulty walking past the concession stand directly into the movie.

❧ I can only hope this advice from Larry Lujack is not too late for you. "When buying a used car, punch the buttons on the radio. If all the stations are rock and roll, there's good chance the transmission is shot."

❧ You might have guessed similar numbers. Seventy six percent of all traffic tickets are given to only 15 percent of all drivers.

❧ Recent events bring to mind this thought from James Thurber, "You can fool too many of the people too much of the time."

❧ A chiromancer is not a romantic chiropractor; a chiromancer is simply a palm reader.

Pass the Blood, Bud

As I recall, my first one was a Schick Collegiate (even though I was just in high school). The electric razor has made life easier and more pleasant for many men (and women).

Joseph Schick invented the modern form of electric razor in 1928, but an early form of razor had been invented 20 years prior to Schick's device.

My cute little electric was doing an adequate job for me until the summer of 1960 when I went to ROTC summer camp at Fort Riley, Kansas. Someone suggested to me that electricity would be hard to come by in that remote location so I left my electric razor home. To my shock on arriving at the post there not only was electricity but also running water.

Undaunted I proceeded to shave with the brand new safety razor— first invented by King Gillette in 1895 and sold in 1903—much to the amusement of my fellow cadet officers. They quickly discovered it was no laughing matter and for the first two weeks of my shaving attempts they always made certain that a friend who also had O-positive blood was standing by. Today, I've stopped the bleeding, and an electric razor is only a stopgap to the real harvest.

Some planets have mottoes. Take Melmac, the home of ALF from the TV show of that name. Melmac's motto was "Are you going to finish that sandwich?" I like it.

🍂 The Checkered Game of Life sounds like something we all play everyday, but it was really the first mass-produced parlor game. Milton Bradley developed it around 1860.

🍂 I believe I can accurately speak for all of us when I say that from time to time we suffer from an outbreak of horripilation. That's the technical term for goosebumps.

🍂 Well, I'll be darned. Electric dishwashers use about 37 percent less water than washing by hand. In addition, prewashing or rinsing the dishes is simply a waste of water in most cases as new dish-washers can handle almost everything but big chunks or bones.

🍂 You know Mother Nature has a sense of fairness (and humor) when you realize that both lions and wildebeest (that's Gnus to you) can run 50 miles per hour.

🍂 Big Brother may be watching you. On a normal day, your name is transmitted between computers at least five times.

🍂 To receive a dual honor like this one, a man had to be authentic. Tex Ritter is the only person enshrined in both the Cowboy Hall of Fame in Oklahoma City and the Country and Western Music Hall of Fame in Nashville. Tex starred in 85 B-westerns and had four songs hit the pop charts in addition to being the first artist to record for Capitol records where he had a number of country hits.

❧ SOS was a real "Johnny-come-lately" as a distress signal. "CQD" (Come—Quick—Danger) was the accepted signal of choice until 1911.

❧ Here's a question for you, when a billing clerk goes off the deep end does he hear strange invoices?

❧ Robert Benchley advises us that dogs are good for boys with this thought. "A dog teaches a boy fidelity, perseverance and to turn around three times before lying down." Twoey and I do this at naptime.

❧ Don't they all look alike and just dress differently? If a girl owns one Barbie she probably owns a total of seven according to research findings.

❧ Where do they get these names? The code name for the hokey U.S. invasion of Grenada was Operation Urgent Fury.

❧ That phrase "meet a deadline" has a real finality to it. To us it means finish a project or activity on time. When it originated in the 1860s it was in the context of Civil War prisoner of war camps. Many had no fences due to lack of resources so a boundary line was drawn around the camp. If a prisoner crossed the line he was shot. Thus "deadline" had real meaning.

Roller Derby Is Not a Hat

🔊 Jim Croce sang of it; Raquel Welch starred in a movie about it; and even Mickey Rooney starred in an early film extolling its virtues. If you haven't guessed that I'm talking about Roller Derby by now, good for you. You've kept your entertainment choices at a slightly higher level than some have.

In 1935, deep in the middle of the Depression a Chicagoan named Leo Seltzer invented Roller Derby. He trademarked the name, organized teams in the Midwest for his league and watched the sport gather momentum. The rules are simple, a team of five skaters tries to get one of their teammates past the other members of a team of five. Guns, clubs, brass knuckles and weapons of mass destruction are prohibited but anything else goes. After the war Roller Derby picked up again and at the Roller Derby World Series in 1950 Madison Square Garden was packed with more than 16,000 spectators. The sport resembled World Wrestling Foundation on older skates and had its own set of heroes and heroines. The sport peaked in the early '70s (nothing to do with Raquel's movie) and by 1973 the original circuit was gone from television. I haven't seen it on trash sports TV so perhaps it died a well-earned death. If you get tickets to a rerun, don't call.

&. Among those patented inventions whose time has not yet come are a Combination Deer-Carcass Sled and Chaise Lounge, a Fluid-Operated Zipper (you don't want to know), and a Power-Operated Pool Cue Stick. If you're a marketing ace, here are three golden opportunities.

&. I passed a friend and neighbor walking her dog the other morning. She tossed me a greeting of "Just keepin' this old dog alive." I thought a moment and called back, "That's why I run. Just keepin' this old dog alive." Running at a modest pace, six miles an hour, can use 600 calories in an hour. Walking just slightly slower, four miles an hour, will use 300–400 calories in an hour. Both will get your heart rate up and help your metabolism. Let's keep those old dogs alive.

&. There was a Pocahontas. That name meant "playful one" in her native language. Don't get your Johns confused though, she married John Rolfe not John Smith. After she died of smallpox in England her son Thomas was raised and educated in England returning to Virginia as an adult.

&. Independence Day (July 4th) hasn't been kind to our presidents. John Adams and Thomas Jefferson both died on July 4, 1826. They were joined five years to the day later by James Monroe. In addition, Zachary Taylor contracted a fatal illness on July 4th and died five days later.

&. Marvin Albinak finally brought to light the secret of some of the charts I saw in my prior occupation when he said, "When graphing a function, the width of the line should be inversely proportional to the precision of the data."

🕭 Why would a director want a cameo performance of only someone's hands? Perhaps if the hands were those of John Scarne famed gambling expert and he was manipulating the cards instead of Paul Newman in the fabulous film *The Sting*.

🕭 Our word for that spiny little creature, the porcupine, comes from the 15th century French *porc d'espine* meaning "thorny pig."

🕭 I'm still not certain I know where it all comes from. In the average minute 20,900 gallons of water flow from the Amazon River into the Atlantic Ocean.

🕭 Next time you're buying a tie for a loved one—even if that's yourself—note that blue neckties sell the best (are the most popular) while red is second. I guess my pink-dotted one is somewhere down the line.

🕭 The identity of "The Thing" was never revealed, but it probably wasn't the same one. Phil Harris had a big novelty hit in 1950 with "The Thing." One year later James Arness got a break in show business by playing the title role (an 8-foot, carrot-like alien being) in the sci-fi thriller *The Thing*.

🕭 I'm not sure why and I've never seen it as a sport in competition—not sure I want to—but there are fifteen members on a hurling team.

By Any Name
It's Still Flip or Lose

🐝 My friend's machine "Guys and Dolls" certainly wasn't one of the first that was built—the musical hit Broadway in 1950—but it's at the antique level today. The first toy pinball game machine was built in 1910 by Adolph Caillie in Detroit. The Caillie Log Tavern was based on the European game bagatelle. Caillie's featured marbles shot on an inclined board then rolling down through a course with pins set in it. The next innovation occurred in 1931, when David Gottlieb created a version called "Baffle Ball" that had a spring-loaded mechanism to launch the balls and a coin-operation.

Time passed and the first machine with electricity was introduced in 1933.

Bumpers followed in 1937 and the first flippers appeared in 1947. The game continues to evolve as electronics and other assorted games compete for the "gamers" consumer dollars.

My friend's pinball machine is still functioning after he gave it the electrical engineer's overhaul, and it's probably worth a lot more today to collectors than when he got it used at age 15.

Oh yes, the tilt function got its name from an early user who was handling the game roughly and caused it to interrupt the play and then said, "Darn, I tilted it." The manufacturer who was standing nearby changed the name of his device to "Tilt" from "stool pigeon" and altered the play forever.

๖ Is it just me or do you find it strange that after spending billions on paved roads in the United States that thousands of people are purchasing SUVs and four-wheel drive vehicles so they can drive off the road in the dirt?

๖ This is just a word of warning to travelers who might go through New Glarus, Wisconsin at the wrong time. The residents of New Glarus hold a William Tell festival so watch your handling of apples.

๖ I wasn't paying attention when it happened. In 1996, India changed the name of the world's fifth-largest metropolitan area from Bombay to Mumbai. I guess the makers of Bombay Sapphire Gin missed it too. I haven't seen any Mumbai gin.

๖ Concerned about earthquakes? Iowa, Florida, North Dakota and Wisconsin were the only four states to experience no earthquakes for the 20 years from 1975 to 1995. No promises, but Rugby, North Dakota is also the geographic center of the North American continent so it may be very safe.

❧ Here's a challenge for those of you with firm teeth who are young at heart (or just young). The largest bubble ever blown (and recorded) with bubble gum measured 22 inches in diameter.

❧ Perhaps some of the more senior among us can empathize with Jackie Gleason as Ralph Kramden when he said, "Just because I've been married for 25 years is no reason to stop being sexy."

❧ James Shields just liked being a senator. He's the only man to have represented three different states as senator, Illinois 1849–1855, Minnesota 1858–1859 and Missouri 1879.

❧ There are a number of my friends and myself who are struggling with an attack of canities. Some of my woman friends have already coped with it and defeated it (with a little help). Canities is the medical term for graying or whitening of the hair.

❧ How many housewives (and house-husbands) have blessed her name over the last 125-plus years. Susan Hibbard invented the feather duster and patented it in 1876, the same year the Sioux dusted Custer.

❧ I know what a fondue is; they're pretty tasty but a "fondu?" Turns out it's a movement in ballet that is a lowering of the body (kind of like dipping) by bending the knee of the supporting leg.

A Different Type of Hospitality

My granddaughter called it a "hos-table" and she might have been close to describing the first ones. The hospital as we know it dates back to India of 500 B.C. The original institutions stressed cleanliness, proper nutrition and the gentle treatment of patients. The Greeks and then the Romans continued to take the process further and in the Middle Ages monks were the primary hosts of "infirmatoria." The first hospital in the United States was built on Manhattan Island in 1663.

Phoebe Anne Mozee isn't exactly a name that rolls off the tongue when describing western characters, but her stage name Annie Oakley is. A star of Buffalo Bill Cody's Wild West Show, she developed her skill with guns at age nine by shooting the heads off squirrels to help feed her impoverished Ohio family. She married sharpshooter Frank Butler in

1876 when they apparently hit it off together. The Annie Oakley Museum is located in Greenville, Ohio.

🐾 I don't think I'll make any changes in my running based on this. The risk that a jogger will die while running is two and one half deaths per one million hours of running.

🐾 The Ottoman Empire was not a furniture store specializing in cushioned footrests. The empire began as a tiny state in the 14th century but expanded through conquests of neighboring states to its greatest expansion in the 16th century when it included southeastern Europe, the Middle East and North Africa. Wars with other European countries caused it to dwindle during the next two centuries, and in 1922 the Empire's successor emerged as the independent country of Turkey.

🐾 I'll have a good idea when you learned to read if you can tell me the name of Dick and Jane's cat. Yep, it was Puff.

🐾 The name was probably appropriate. The first unofficial presidential airplane was a civilian version of the B-24 Liberator customized for Franklin Roosevelt during World War II. The plane was named the "Guess Where II."

🐾 Other than their claim to great potatoes, Idaho residents can also boast that theirs is the only state in the U.S. over which no foreign flag has flown.

❧ The first U.S. airmail stamp was a picture of a C3A Curtis Jenny Biplane. The stamp cost 24 cents. One sheet was inadvertently produced with the airplane flying upside down. One of those 100 stamps is worth about $36,000. Check your very old letters.

❧ Nigel Rees tells us that "Celibacy is not an inherited characteristic."

❧ He obviously wrote from experience. Meredith Wilson, creator of "The Music Man," was once a soloist with John Phillip Sousa's marching band.

❧ You coulda' guessed it. The only contestant to quit after the first question on the TV show "The $64,000 Question" was Jack Benny. Benny's category was violins and after identifying the famous 18th century violinmaker whose first name was Antonio with Stradivari, Benny quit with $64. What's more, he refused to leave the stage until emcee Hal March took the money out of his own pocket and handed it to him.

❧ Anagrams, words or phrases whose letters can be rearranged to create another word or phrase, are fun, especially if the second is similar in meaning to the first. Try this: SNOOZE ALARMS becomes ALAS! NO MORE Z'S.

❧ The names sound like members of a rock group you wouldn't want to listen to, but Slimy Gomphidus, Inky Cap, Sulphur Top, Pig's Ears and Shaggy Mane are the names of mushrooms. You might not want to test another sense and eat them either.

A Mustang Gathering By Any Other Name Is Still A Roundup

❧ Everywhere you looked you saw Mustangs. No, I'm not talking about one of those great B-westerns from the 1940s and early '50s. I'm referring to a classic car rally featuring just Ford Mustangs. The entire main street of Steamboat Springs, Colorado was parked wall-to-wall and end-to-end with the shiniest cars I've ever seen.

Ford Motor Company introduced the first Mustang, the 1965 model, in advance of the normal model year in April of 1964. The car took off, literally and figuratively. First year sales totaled 680,000 units of the three basic models, two-door hardtop, convertible and fastback. This car was supposedly Lee Iacocca's baby and he must have been a proud papa.

The rally had the cars parked by vintage so you could watch the engineering changes evolve. The intriguing aspect of the whole affair was that most of the cars were in better shape than their owners of the same vintage were.

❧ I don't remember the face, but the roar is familiar. Metro-Goldwyn-Mayer (MGM) adopted the lion as their symbol because their publicity director at that time was Howard Dietz. Dietz graduated from Columbia University whose nickname was the Lions and whose football song was "Roar, Lion, Roar."

❧ That familiar "RX" on your prescriptions is there because it's the Latin abbreviation for "recipe." Funny, I didn't even know my friendly doctor spoke Latin. He's never spoken to me in it.

❧ Could you believe someone who said he was a member of the Ananias Club? I don't know. That's the club of which all members are liars.

❧ If you saw a collection of herons, would you know to call it a siege? That's the appropriate collective word just like a group of swans is a wedge.

❧ I simply had to share one of my favorite movie quotes. "In Italy, for thirty years under the Borgias, they had warfare, terror, murder and bloodshed, but they produced Michelangelo, Leonardo da Vinci and the Renaissance. In Switzerland, they had brotherly love, they had 500 years of democracy and peace—and what did they produce? The cuckoo clock." The great Orson Welles as Harry Lime spoke those lines in the 1949 film noir classic, *The Third Man*.

❧ There are days when your kids or grandkids are down with a bad case of didaskaleinophobia. That's the abnormal fear of going to school. It may peak on test days.

🐾 The way things have been going, maybe they should have stayed in Portsmouth. The Detroit Lions made their entrance to the National Football League as the Portsmouth Spartans in 1930. When the team moved to Detroit in 1934 they became the Lions.

🐾 Greg Risberg, a social worker, offers this bit of advice, "Four hugs a day are the minimum needed to meet a person's 'skin hunger.'"

🐾 Undecennial sounds like it would be an underwear celebration but no, it merely means every 11 years. Sorry.

🐾 Thousands of young boys owned a set of electric trains made by Joshua Cowen. He invented the toy electric train around 1900. He used his middle name for the name of his company, Lionel.

🐾 Here's a variation on the "Tom Swifty" called "The Croaker" by its inventor Roy Bongartz. *I hate sweet potatoes,*" Tom yammered.

🐾 Walter Winchell came up with a very clever euphemism. He referred to the term pregnant as "infanticipating."

🐾 Along those same lines: "Show me a twin birth and I'll show you an infant replay." –Bob Phillips.

Monk-eying Around?

🐝 Have you been spending your "Mendelian Inheritance"? You may have without even being aware of it if you have children. "Mendelian Inheritance" refers to genetic traits carried through heredity. Austrian monk Gregor Mendel studied and described the process in the 19th century. He was the first to deduce correctly the basic principles of heredity, but he needed a good press agent and English biologist William Bateson filled that role as he brought Mendel's work to the attention of the scientific world. Bateson also coined the term "genetics." Note—this does not describe how your kids can drive you temporarily insane.

🐝 Success breeds more success. On his first voyage, Christopher Columbus was entrusted by Ferdy and Izzie with three ships. On his second junket he had seventeen under his command. Some of the other fourteen were undoubtedly early cruise ships.

🐝 You could say Bond always had an eye for the "birds" if you were a Brit. Ian Fleming took the name of his sophisticated spy from a coffee-table book, "Birds of the West Indies" by ornithologist, James Bond.

 Surprises happen when you think you know something and you find out you don't. If I asked you where the term "rub out" came from, you'd probably say gangsters of the 1920s. Then I'd tell you that the term came from the early 19th century trappers who translated it from the plains Indians sign language for "to kill" which was indicated by a rubbing motion. Surprise.

 "See ya later Alligator." The only place outside the Southeastern United States where alligators occur naturally is the Yangtze-Kiang river basin in eastern China. These smaller Chinese cousins are rapidly becoming extinct. All other large mouthed saurians are either crocodiles or caimans.

 I like Salvador Dali's explanation. "The reason that some portraits don't look true to life is that some people make no effort to resemble their pictures."

 Just pairing "Kukla, Fran and Ollie" with the Boston Pops and Arthur Fiedler would be special, but the real reason this 1953 show was so special was that NBC made it the first nationwide TV broadcast in color.

 It's food for ugly speculation. Humans and pigs are the only two animals that sunburn.

 Some days it would be good to have one around. Remember that little (fictitious) animal in the "Li'l Abner" comic strip that liked to have aggressions taken out on it? It was the "Kigmy."

❧ The newspaper headline that celebrated Douglas "Wrong Way" Corrigan's flight to Ireland in 1938 read "NAGIR-ROC YAWGNORW OT LIAH."

❧ Here's some more help for those difficult performance evaluation comments. "The wheel is turning, but the hamster is dead." And "When she opens her mouth, it seems that it is only to change feet."

❧ I wonder if this counts the times they keep your coins without providing any goodies. An average American will spend more than $6,800 on vending machines in a lifetime.

❧ Census results show that U.S. men live the longest in the Pacific states (Oregon, Washington, California, Alaska and Hawaii) and U.S. women live the longest in the southern states of Kentucky, Tennessee, Mississippi and Alabama. Maybe the survivors can meet in Kansas.

❧ Well, pin a rose on it. Walter Hunt invented the safety pin in 1849.

❧ She had a good run for a time. Bette Claire Graham invented "white out," the fluid used to correct typewriter mistakes. She founded her own company to manufacture the stuff in 1956.

❧ Number, please! The first pay telephone was installed in 1899 in Hartford, Connecticut .

In the Know About Crows

&. What is there about crows that fascinates so many of us? Crows are among the smartest of birds. Their groups, called murders, post sentinels when they eat. They seem to leave roadkill at precisely the right time to avoid becoming more. Roman civilization regarded the crow as a symbol of the future for its cry "Cras, Cras" (tomorrow, tomorrow).

Thornton Burgess the wonderful author of the *Mother West Wind* children's stories featured "Blackie the Crow" as one of his major characters. "The Fox and the Crow" rated their own comics in the '40s and '50s.

Crows and their big cousins Ravens belong to the family "Corvidae" and their subfamily is "Corvinae" which classifies them generally as songbirds. I'm OK with that if your songs run toward blues and lyrics like "Nevermore."

Crows are even part of our metaphors with "eating crow" being an expression for doing something really disagreeable. Actually, according to noted ornithologist John James Audubon crow doesn't taste all that bad. I'm not going to say kind of like chicken. So, perhaps all of this may elevate your opinion of the crow as a worthwhile contributor to the ecology or you may just echo "Nevermore."

🕭 He probably wasn't asked to smile and say "cheese." James Knox Polk was the 11th president of the United States but the very first to be photographed. John Plumbe, the photographer, was also the first to take a picture of the White House.

🕭 I've always liked the color blue myself. During the Ming Dynasty (1368–1644) no one but the reigning emperor was allowed to wear the color green because of its association with jade and emerald. The penalty was more than just being named a fashion outcast; it was death.

🕭 Louisiana has a unique distinction. It's the only state where you can order a meal of Cajun-prepared state crustacean. The crawfish is officially designated as the state crustacean.

🕭 The first stethoscope arose from a case of modesty, not on the part of the patient but on the part of the doctor. In 1816, a French physician, René Laennec was consulted by a young woman whose symptoms suggested heart disease. Laennec couldn't bring himself to place his ear next to her naked chest so he rolled up a newspaper and listened to her heart through it. When he discovered it magnified the sounds he constructed a one-foot cylinder of wood, the first stethoscope. We can probably guess that not all of the 19th century physicians greeted his invention with enthusiasm.

🐾 Naming them after him was a dubious honor at best. K-rations, those delightful little packets of food containing the essential nutrients for soldiers in the field were named after Ancel Keys, an American physiologist. No information is available as to the extent of his gratitude.

🐾 In an unrelated but appropriate comment, Frank Muir described muesli as "a dish that always looks like the sweepings from a better table."

🐾 If it's not one thing it's another. Alaska is the safest state in which to live relative to the risk per capita of dying from heart disease or cancer. Unfortunately, it's the riskiest state to die from an accident.

🐾 When F. W. Woolworth opened his chain of "dime stores" in England in 1909, they were called "Three-and-Sixpence" stores.

🐾 Real baseball fans can easily quote Babe Ruth's home run record but few would recall that his major league pitching record was 94 wins against 46 losses, not a bad percentage.

🐾 Perhaps his number was 007 and a half? James Bond had an older brother named Henry in the novels by Ian Fleming. Bond, Henry Bond just doesn't have the same dramatic impact does it?

What Do Sailors Know?

🍃 There's a grain of truth in some of the old adages. Take "Red Sky at morning, sailor take warning; red sky at night, sailor's delight," for example. The morning sun glows red because the atmosphere refracts its rays toward the red end of the spectrum, but if it's cloudy, the light can't be seen meaning there may be foul weather coming in from the east. A red glow at sunset indicates clear weather coming from the east for the next morn. In a remotely related item, Richard Bradford's book, *Red Sky at Morning* is a great read.

🍃 It was in 1970 that the folks at Whirlpool inflicted trash compactors on the American public. Some people used the compactors to sidestep recycling since the devices crunched a lot of stuff together. Satirist Marshal Effron cut to the quick with this comment, "The trash compactor is an invention that takes 50 pounds of garbage and gives you back 50 pounds of garbage."

ঌ One out of two isn't bad. The Edsel (Ford) named after Henry's grandson in 1957 still rings a bell for its number of defects and has become a synonym for an automobile that doesn't work. Edsel Ford, to his greater credit also has the Edsel Ford Range in Antarctica named after him.

ঌ We can credit Major Pierre-Charles L'Enfant for our practice of numbering and lettering our streets (Fifth and Main). He laid out the plans for Washington, D.C. using that concept in 1791.

ঌ If you're into capturing large snakes, consider having one person for every four or five feet of python, anaconda or boa constrictor. Or, skip it, have a beer and watch "Animal Planet."

ঌ A very funny man coined our well-used word "nerd." Theodor Geisel was that clever guy. You probably remember him as Dr. Seuss since that was his middle name.

ঌ The difference between poultry and fowl is more than just spelling. Poultry are domesticated fowl. So, chickens are poultry, but ducks may have a choice to make.

ঌ Sounds like a crummy way to do it, but before rubber came into use bread was used to erase lead pencil marks.

ঌ They probably called him a sissy. Charles C. Waitt of Boston is the first player credited with wearing a baseball glove. The year was 1875.

🐾 Got a copy of it? "What Goes On" is the only Beatle song containing lyrics written by John Lennon, Paul McCartney and George Harrison. They let Ringo sing the lead. Sadly, it failed to hit the Top 40.

🐾 Celebrate New Year's Eve on March 20? You do if your calendar follows the astrological year, which begins on March 21 (or if you're a real procrastinator).

🐾 Niels Bohr, a pretty good physicist in his day, defined an expert as "a person who has made all the mistakes that can be made in a very narrow field."

🐾 Toponymy is the study of place names. I won't hazard a guess as to what Bottonymy is the study of.

🐾 Thanks Myron and Esther. A good memory is an inherited trait.

🐾 "Rosie the Riveter" was real! At the least the woman in the World War II poster was based on the work done by an aircraft worker named Rosita Bonavita who with a co-worker placed 3,345 rivets in the wing of a Grumman Avenger torpedo bomber during a six-hour shift.

🐾 Certainly as far as horses go it was big-time. Secretariat was the winner of the Triple Crown of racing in 1973. *Time, Newsweek* and *Sports Illustrated* all featured him on their covers in the same week. Word is he enjoyed the next stage of his career.

The Screen Size Was Small, The Entertainment Large

Early television was fascinating for more than just the novelty of the large box with the tiny picture. One of my particular favorites—maybe one of yours if you're the right age—was "The Colgate Comedy Hour." The first telecast took place on September 10, 1950, and the show finally collapsed under the weight of its budget in December of 1955. The show gave visibility to such comic greats as Abbott and Costello, Eddie Cantor, Martin and Lewis, Bob Hope and Donald O'Connor as guest hosts.

The Comedy Hour was also the first commercial series to originate in Hollywood. The show at times featured musicals such as "Anything Goes" with Ethel Merman and Frank Sinatra and "Roberta" with Gordon MacRae. The program even traveled around the country for special events, but the emphasis remained on big names and big shows.

The final edition of one of TV's most notable early comedy-variety programs showcased Fred Waring and his Pennsylvanians from Hollywood on December 25 with Christmas music. Clink, here's to its passing from the entertainment stage.

❧ Tourists wouldn't necessarily flock to a community known as "Porkopolis" so perhaps that's why Cincinnati downplayed its nickname in the 1830s. The city was famous for its hog industry at the time.

❧ According to some authorities, the five most persuasive words in the English language are: results, easy, guarantee, discover and health. I might suggest another, free.

❧ File this under the category of unique and special. There's a green grocer named Nick in the mountains outside of Brisbane, Queensland Australia who does a great Elvis impersonation. Nick's alter ego is Elvis Parsley and his establishment is "Grapeland." If you're lucky he will enter (in costume) to the strains of "Also Sprach Zarathustra" as Elvis did and launch into "C.C. Rider" frequently Elvis's first number. Nick uses a carrot in addition to his real microphone and does requests like "Don't Be Cruel" for the customers that like to dance. I happened to enjoy the performance not long ago and lingered long enough to buy some excellent fresh fruit.

❧ If you're female and in the market for a new relationship you might take this advice from Rita Rudner. She said, "To attract men I wear a perfume called 'New Car Interior'."

🐌 I suppose it's a statement of where we've come as a society these days. In a recent poll roughly two of every five American kids named a movie star as their hero. "Where have you gone Joe Dimaggio?"

🐌 Products get their names in interesting ways. Take the cigarette brand "Lucky Strikes." Dr. R. A. Patterson, a doctor from Virginia, used the name to attract miners to the tobacco he sold during the California Gold Rush in the 1850s. We don't know if he was a specialist in respiratory diseases.

🐌 I suppose we could claim sex discrimination, but maybe it has to do with who's driving. Seventy-one percent of car accident victims are male, 29 percent are female.

🐌 Here's a suggestion for a change in breakfast menus. An ice cream bar is 20 percent sugar while Sugar Smacks cereal is 61 percent sugar. Sure, it'll be cold on the teeth but tasty with coffee.

🐌 It makes sense to me. Our word "tax" comes from the Latin word meaning "touch sharply."

🐌 Carrying one around your neck is bad; shooting one in a British golf game is good. The British use the word albatross to indicate three under par on a single hole similar to the U.S. double eagle.

🐌 Got any friends like this? If you peer into one side a gecko's ear, you can see clear through to the other side.

Tunes For the Road

🎵 What would a car be like without its own radio? Paul Galvin couldn't believe that the auto had existed for more than two decades without tunes so he invented the car radio in 1929. The device was about the size of a large toolbox and had a speaker installed under the car's floorboards. The sound wasn't great but the radio was a commercial success. Galvin proceeded to found the Motorola Company.

So today when a car pulls up along side of you at a stoplight and is vibrating with noise like it was a rolling speaker just remember to thank Paul Galvin.

🎵 I don't have a ghost writer, but many others have. The term dates to the late 1890s but the practice apparently existed as far back as Caesar's time (his secretary probably wrote the *Veni, vidi, vici* line). Mark Twain wrote most of Ulysses S. Grant's "autobiography." Having a ghostwriter makes it harder to "eat your own words."

🐚 There are at least 100,000 chemical reactions occurring in the normal human brain every second. You can only guess at how many are occurring in yours or in the average high school student's in Chemistry class.

🐚 You certainly can't compare them to couch potatoes. The average bear loses up to one fourth of its body weight during hibernation.

🐚 It's hard to even imagine it now, but popcorn was banned in many movie theaters in the 1920s because it was too noisy. That was before "talkies."

🐚 Here's a bit of trivia for you. Robert Ripley (*Believe It or Not*) was the first inductee into the National Trivia Hall of Fame.

🐚 The first presidential jogger was none other than Teddy Roosevelt. He jogged around the Washington Monument daily. Teddy is considered the most athletic of all the presidents.

🐚 This Chinese proverb may say something to us about our National Parks and Monuments: "The one who removed the mountain was the one who began carrying away stones."

🐚 I'm still collecting those country-western song lyrics because I love phrasing like this: "When she said she was sleepy, I knew she was tired of me." And "She dumped me for the garbage man."

🐚 I finally outgrew this one (I think). If you play basketball regularly, the odds are one in 40 you will be injured playing in any given year.

❧ Antarctica is the only continent to be truly "discovered" since no one was living there when it was found. The continent is centered on the South Pole and lies almost entirely within the Antarctic Circle.

❧ Remember this one from 1950?
>   HER CHARIOT
>   RACED 80 PER
>   THEY HAULED AWAY
>   WHAT HAD
>   BEN HUR
>   BURMA SHAVE

❧ Here's some more research I hope we didn't fund. Most earthworms like to eat ice cream.

❧ "The natives are restless tonight ..." I've said it myself upon appropriate occasions (some related to children). Charles Laughton said it first in the 1933 movie *The Island of Lost Souls.*

❧ I'm struggling with the picture of him saying to children, "Hey kids, what time is it?" Robert Goulet played Timber Tom, host of the Canadian edition of the TV show, "Howdy Doody Time" when it was introduced in 1954.

❧ The statistic is a sad one. Over the last 3,500 years, the world has been at peace about one month out of every year (8 percent of the time).

It Was a Model Life

❧ Other boys with ten thumbs will relate to my difficulty. I had a terrible time with those balsa model airplane kits. The first balsa-wood kits appeared in the 1920s capitalizing on the glamour of air combat in World War I between Spads and Fokkers.

When World War II arrived, the kits became more sophisticated and sanding was required on the wooden model kits of Mustangs, Spitfires and Zeros. I wasn't good at that nor at the delicate painting required after assembly. Someone must have been thinking of me for in the early '50s the first plastic model airplane kits were marketed. At last, something I could snap together with airplane cement that actually looked like a real plane. I doted

on Sabre Jets and Grumman Panthers and even had a Mig-15 as the Korean War was in full swing.

The plastic planes were mostly for show or zooming around with your hands while the early balsa models were propelled by rubber-band motors or in a few cases by two-cycle gasoline engines. Plastic kits have kept pace with modern aircraft, but the few of my models that remain are more than antiques; they're memories.

🐾 Little Red Riding Hood's first name was not "Little." In the original fairy tale she was named Blanchette.

🐾 Farmers can blame that extra hour of daylight on none other than Benjamin Franklin. Ben came up with the concept of Daylight Savings Time.

🐾 It's a lot faster and more entertaining than watching grass grow. Bamboo is the fastest growing plant on earth and can grow as much as 35 inches in one day.

🐾 There's a slight chance there are honor graduates among you. The very first correspondence course in tree surgery was offered by Davey Tree Expert Company of Kent Ohio in 1914. I wonder how a tree goes about getting a second opinion.

🐾 Wilson Mizner offers some important advice to men of my generation, "When a woman tells you her age it's alright to look surprised, but don't scowl."

🐾 Agent 007 is certainly the most famous British secret agent in film or fiction. Few would know Agent 002, Phil Fairbanks, James' friend in the novels by Ian Fleming.

🐾 Among those characters passed by time is Andy Panda. Walter Lantz created the little guy in a 1939 cartoon, "Life Begins for Andy Panda." Andy hit paper in 1941 in "Crackajack Funnies No.39." His girlfriend was Miranda Panda, and they lived in Pandamania.

❧ The name even sounds long. The Trans-Siberian Railroad is the longest railroad in the world. Czar Alexander III launched the building of the railroad that would join eastern and western Russia in 1891. The railroad was finally opened in 1904.

❧ We're revolting so we need a new calendar. The National Convention devised a new calendar in 1793 as a result of the French Revolution's attempt to rid French society of Christian influences.

The calendar did have 12 months but each was composed of three *de'cades* and each *de'cade* was composed of ten days. When Napoleon came in to power in 1806, he said enough; if I'm going to conquer other countries I want to know what calendars they're using. No he didn't, I made that part up, but he did cause France to revert to the Gregorian Calendar.

❧ In a very remotely related item, in a lifetime the average American will receive more than 2,300 greeting cards of which 524 will be birthday cards (many of those will be nasty and snide).

❧ Maybe it's your turn tomorrow. On any particular day, one half of the world's population will eat rice.

❧ Talk about hypocritical. Mary Louise Alcott did not like little girls. She wrote *Little Women* out of greed. She wanted the bucks. I really don't know about "Little Men."

A Concert for the Ages

❧ I missed Elvis in concert, the Beatles, too. I didn't really want to see Michael Jackson, but let me tell you about the concert I'm really sorry I missed. It took place on January 16, 1938 (a little too early for me). The setting was Carnegie Hall. The artists were the famous Benny Goodman Band: Benny on clarinet, Harry James and Ziggy Elman on trumpets, Gene Krupa on drums, Red Ballard and Vernon Brown on trombones, Jess Stacy on piano and a host of other musical greats. The highlight of the evening was the band's rendition of "Sing, Sing, Sing (With a Swing)" – I'm listening to it as I type. The event marked the real recognition of swing and jazz in American music. Rock and Roll would have to wait until 1955 for its opportunity.

❧ There was a real "Dr. Pepper." Wade Morrison, who created the drink in 1885, chose to name his new concoction after

Dr. Charles Pepper, a Virginia drugstore owner. It seems Dr. Pepper gave Wade his first employment opportunity, and when Wade got his own drugstore and invented a special new drink he thought to honor his first employer.

&. If you think of the Spring season it will probably lead you into remembering the names of Daisy Duck's three nieces. Yup, they were April, May and June.

&. Like the vice presidents themselves, it's pretty easy to overlook the fact that New York was the birthplace of more vice presidents than any other state. Eight veeps were born in the Empire State.

&. "What's up, Duce?" Apparently, Donald Duck was Benito Mussolini's favorite cartoon character. Yeah, I know Bugs Bunny was the "What's up, Doc" guy, but I couldn't pass up the pun.

&. Perhaps he just wasn't paying attention. Abel Tasman discovered Tasmania (it figures), New Zealand and Fiji but didn't stumble onto Australia.

&. "Tea for Two" would be seven and a half. The average British citizen drinks 3¾ cups of tea per day.

&. The word "Jeopardy" wasn't invented by Alex Trebek or Merv Griffin, who invented the TV show. The root was the French chess term *jeu parti* (from the 13th century) meaning "a divided play or game." It thus came to mean uncertainty and emerged in the late 16th century in its present spelling.

❧ If you're wicket wacky you probably already know that the U.S. Croquet Hall of Fame is located in Palm Beach Gardens, Florida. Notable enshrinees include Harpo Marx and Samuel Goldwyn.

❧ "Aaah, ooo-ahhh." The first athlete to swim 100 meters in less than a minute was Johnny Weissmuller. He accomplished the feat in July of 1922.

❧ Here's an update on that "canal palindrome": "A man, a plan, a cat, a ham, a yak, a yam, a hat, a canal: Panama."

❧ The fastest rabbits can run about 35 miles an hour, and the fastest greyhounds can step it out at 39.4 miles an hour. Is it any wonder those dogs at the race tracks chase the mechanical rabbits? They just know they can't keep up that pace.

❧ Now I know my problem. Vic Braden, tennis instructor, once said, "My theory is that if you buy an ice cream cone and make it hit your mouth you can play. If you stick it on your forehead your chances are less." It's tough getting ice cream out of your eyebrows.

❧ You might not think this, but Antarctica is the driest continent on the planet. The continent receives less than two inches of precipitation annually. The ice has been there for thousands of years.

❧ The "Dark Continent" (Africa) is 28 percent wilderness. North America is 38 percent wilderness, thanks to our neighbors to the north and south.

Well, Stick My Bumper

❧ "Ever stop to think, and forget to start again?" and "A Blast from the Past, WALL DRUG" are classic examples of the bumper sticker which has become such a part of American culture. Not long after World War II fluorescent ink and self-sticking adhesive were developed. In that window of time, a company called Gill-line, that had been founded in 1934 and specialized in printing and decorating canvas products, combined the ink and self-sticking adhesive to produce a sign that could be easily affixed to a car bumper. Earlier bumper signs had been attached with wire, but this was the first "sticker." When Gill-line hit its 50th anniversary in 1984, it had already manufactured more than a billion bumper stickers.

Today, we're all fascinated and eager to read the latest clever saying even though some transcend the boundaries of good taste. I prefer the clever over the disgusting, but then I've always loved the wit of words.

❧ Well, there you go then. The English Horn is not English, and in fact, it's not a horn. It's a form of oboe that was developed in France.

🔊 Vermont, the Green Mountain State, came by its monicker rightfully. "Vert" is French for "green" and "mont" means "mountain."

🔊 This wouldn't give me a warm feeling, literally. The capital of Bolivia, La Paz, is so high (more than 12,000 feet above sea level) and has so little oxygen that fires struggle to stay lit. For years, the city had no fire department.

🔊 Curious about that expression "the naked truth?" It came from an ancient legend where Truth and Falsehood went bathing in a stream. When Falsehood came out of the water she dressed in Truth's clothing and ran away. Truth was unwilling to wear Falsehood's clothing and went "naked."

🔊 I didn't know that. The seven points in the crown of the Statue of Liberty represent the seven continents.

🔊 The Accounting Hall of Fame is located in Columbus, Ohio. For the number cruncher fans among us it's a chance to see those great accountants of the past like…well, I'll come up with someone. I do know of a firm whose members probably won't make the cut.

🔊 Yale was the very first university in the U.S. to adopt a mascot. Their choice was a bulldog named Handsome Dan. I could conjure up a Bichon Frise with that name but probably not a bulldog.

🙐 Boing! Boing! Boing! George Hansburg invented the pogo stick in 1919. I'm uncertain of his motivation, but he must have had something in mind.

🙐 On more than one occasion I've noticed a person—mostly male—with a very limited nasion. You know the nasion, that space between the eyebrows. Any other conclusions I'd draw might not be valid in all cases.

🙐 You might deduce with some good reason that a nephometer would be a counter or measurement device for nephews. Not so, it's an instrument used for measuring the amount of cloud cover in the sky.

🙐 Bill Bradley, ex-U.S. Senator and New York Knick, expressed an opinion I share when he spoke of a 20-year-old teammate's idea of making a movie of his life. He said, "Only one 20-year-old was ever worth making a movie about. That was Mozart."

🙐 Sports guys say funny things. Danny Murtaugh, ex-Pittsburgh Pirates manager once commented, "Why, certainly I'd like to have a fellow who hits a home run every time at bat, who strikes out every opposing batter when he's pitching, and who is always thinking about two innings ahead. The only trouble is to get him to put down his beer, come down out of the stands and do those things."

🙐 Wars do cost money. To pay for the costs of the Civil War, President Abraham Lincoln signed an income tax into law.

Bridge Across Untroubled Water

❧ To be sure, there were many accidental ones but the first true bridge as we know it was constructed across the Euphrates River in Babylon in 700 B.C. The structure was made of logs secured together with twine and lasted for many decades. As you might guess, the Romans were the most successful of the early bridge builders because of their engineering skills and concepts of architectural design. In 50 B.C. Julius Caesar gave an order to bridge the Rhine River and ten days later a 1,378-foot bridge was in place. It's good to be the emperor.

❧ Presidential anecdotes are great! The late Harry Truman peppered many of his talks with colorful terms as many might remember. After the birth of his first grandchild, he told his daughter, "When he gets older, I'm going to teach him to talk." "The hell you are!" Margaret responded.

❧ The fresh ones from Alaska are the best. I'm talking about the largest of the flat fish, the Halibut. In old England, the common name for any flat fish was "butt." The most highly regarded fish was reserved for eating on holy days, and they named it the "haly butt" for haly was the old-time spelling of holy. Today we eat it on any day, and halibut no longer means "holy flounder."

🐾 The naming is certainly understandable. Separation Creek in Oregon flows between two mountains known as The Husband and The Wife. It must have been successful. There are no small foothills nearby named The Kids.

🐾 Could a beauty known as Helen of Hissarlik have a "face that launched a thousand ships"? I think not. However, Hissarlik is the Turkish site supposedly laid over ancient Troy.

🐾 A tan tern is not that unusual. The Arctic Tern travels from pole to pole twice a year. The "sunbird" enjoys nearly four months of continuous daylight in each of the Arctic and Antarctic summers. The journey is about a 20,000-mile roundtrip.

🐾 If you're an average American, you'll write around 15,000 checks in your lifetime. Unfortunately, about one percent of them bounce. Our creditors will be calling later.

🐾 "The General Electric College Bowl" had its inception in 1959 as host Allen Ludden asked questions of two teams of college students. The popularity of the program lead to the University of Colorado founding a trivia bowl in 1968 as the TV College Bowl was fading.

🐾 Try this one next time. It's Paul Fussell's suggested response to the incredibly overused "Have a nice day." He said, "Thank you, but I have other plans."

🍃 Our word "lingerie" is derived from the French word of the same spelling. The French term of derivation was *linge* meaning linen. In my experience (which is limited), the sleepwear and other forms of intimate apparel currently denoted by the word are no longer made of linen.

🍃 He must have liked it set to music. "Who could ask for anything more" was a phrase used by Ira Gershwin in three different songs: "I Got Rhythm" from *Girl Crazy*, "I'm About to Become a Mother" in *Of Thee I Sing* and "Nice Work If You Can Get It" from *Damsel in Distress*. With the Gershwins' music it was hard to "ask for anything more."

🍃 The pumpkin is a product of limited usage. More than 99 percent of them sold in the United States wind up as jack-o-lanterns. The "fresh pumpkin" pie is a thing of the past.

🍃 There's at least one at any party of reasonable size. We'd call him (or her) a macrologist. No, this is not an expert in macro-biology or macroeconomics, although it could be. A macrologist is someone who engages in long and tiresome talk.

🍃 Here's some food for thought. Today's average consumers wear more computing power on their wrists than existed in the entire world before 1961.

It's Not John Wayne In a Tutu

I may be tiptoeing into dangerous territory here since we have almost as many Richard Simmons videotapes as we do John Wayne videos, but I think it's time we checked into aerobics. Dr. Kenneth Cooper, a U.S. Air Force major with a doctorate in exercise physiology came up with the concept in 1968 because he was directed to come up with some drills for flabby flyboys. Cooper's idea was simple enough, an exercise program (jogging, swimming, bicycling, any sustained exertion) that induced the body to consume at least 50 milliliters of oxygen in 12 minutes.

This was perhaps the biggest breakthrough in fitness since Yale football coach Walter Camp came up with the Daily Dozen in 1920s (been there, done that before Cooper). Cooper's ideas—and books—moved along swimmingly until 1971 when Jacki Sorensen, a dancer from Malibu, led the first aerobics dance class. Wow, now we had exercise and togetherness coupled with hot music. Americans loved it, and fashion was not far behind.

The business of aerobics and fitness clothing has boomed, and now many people wear clothing in public that was formerly limited to the basement or bedroom. Dr. Cooper's revenge will come, of course, when the snapback of spandex will zap those people who just shouldn't wear it.

🙠 In what for some is surely a related item. In a normal lifetime, the average of we Americans will lose 5,126 gallons of perspiration (men sweat, women glow).

🙠 There's only one state among our 50 that is entirely bordered on both the east and west by rivers. If you guessed Iowa you got. The "M's" Missouri and Mississippi mark its western and eastern boundaries respectively.

🙠 "That looks like a Mallard," Tom said seductively.

🙠 We can all hope. French conductor Pierre Monteax commented in an inter-view on his 89th birthday when asked what he enjoyed in life. "I still have two abiding passions. One is my model rail-way, the other—women. But at the age of 89 I find I am getting just a little too old for model railways."

🙠 Curious about those pub names in England, ones like The Green Man and the French Horn or The Golden Dove? It's common sense really. Pubs came into existence before most of the populous could read (going in, coming out would have been even trickier) and drawing a picture of Alastair's Pub was much more difficult than a picture of a sword and a plume or some other interesting identifi-cation. Today, those names are a reminder of the antiquity of the pub.

🐾 The "doggy toupee'" market is probably very busy there (they make the toupee's with adhesive which attaches to the dogs' heads). Dogs in Tokyo have a very high baldness rate apparently because they lead very stressful lives. Now that's sad! Twoey doesn't need one.

🐾 Giraffes can actually go longer without water than camels, but when they gargle it takes a lot more water.

🐾 Smoking kills. In a bad publicity move, R.J. Reynolds paid Amelia Earhart to take "Lucky Strikes" with her on her ill-fated trip across the Pacific.

🐾 His first name escapes history, but the term he inspired lives on. Mr. Scheuster was a crooked criminal lawyer in New York in the middle of the 19th century. His name inspired our word "shyster."

🐾 The rhyming scheme would have been very different. The original—working title—of Irving Berlin's "Alexander's Ragtime Band" was "Alexander and His Clarinet."

🐾 I wonder how it fit with the Boy Scout Oath. Robert Baden Powell, founder of the Boy Scouts in 1908, served as a British spy against both Germany and Russia in the First World War.

🐾 I missed the grand opening, and I'll bet you did too. The White Horse Tavern built in Newport, Rhode Island in 1673 is the oldest tavern in the United States.

The U.N. Near Mount Rushmore?

❧ Oh, what might have been! Few people would note or recall that in the 1940s the Black Hills of South Dakota were in the running for the location of the United Nations headquarters. The Hills were equally accessible by air from Pacific Rim and European countries. South Dakota offered to cede sovereignty of a ten-square-mile piece of the Black Hills creating a "District of the World." Greece endorsed the idea, then the Rockefellers countered with a little bit of Manhattan and the opportunity was gone. It's just as well, Paha Sapa was a sacred peaceful place, and the U.N. wouldn't have been a good fit.

❧ You've heard people say, "We're going to have a meeting of the minds" when they're intending a big business discussion, but did you ever see one Steve Allen arranged? From 1977 to 1981, Allen hosted a number of shows on PBS featuring many of the greatest minds of the past. Characters such as Moses, Ben Franklin, Cleopatra, and Genghis Khan gathered around a kitchen table to exchange ideas.

All characters dressed in period clothes and spoke English using concepts taken from their own writings or historical context. It was a rare experience enhanced by Allen's talents.

🐾 Few bowlers know this (but real math guys would). A bowling pin needs to tilt at least seven and one half degrees to fall. How far an inebriated bowler has to tilt before falling is under research.

🐾 The "S and P" you see set on most American dinner tables is of course, salt and pepper. In Hungary, it's typically salt and paprika.

🐾 Keeping up with the Suzukis? Suzuki is the most common last name in Japan.

🐾 Beware of skunks doing cute little tricks! Spotted skunks do their own version of a "handstand" (pawstand) before they loose their scented spray.

🐾 Don't knock the Bach. The Toys 1965 hit "A Lover's Concerto" was based on "Minuet in G" by Johann Sebastian Bach.

🐾 You've naturally heard of the "terrible twos" but the "terrible threes"? When he was three years old, Ivan the Terrible became Grand Prince of Moscow.

🐾 Some oldtimers still say "Puttin' on the dog" as an expression for assuming airs or making pretensions of grandeur in dress and behavior. The term comes from American college slang of the 1860s. It's probable the term referred to the Blenheim and King Charles spaniels, which were at the height of aristocratic popularity and appeared to be snooty or high-toned dogs.

🐾 If I weren't fairly confident, I'd be reluctant to try this paraphrase of a quote by Drake Sather: "My wife says I never listen to her. At least I think that's what she said."

🐾 Martha cashed it in on September 1, 1914 in Cincinnati (at the zoo). Martha was the last of three to five billion passenger pigeons that once lived in eastern North America. In the early 1800s, passenger pigeons were the world's most abundant bird. Over-hunting triggered a chain of events leading to their downfall. Extinct means forever.

🐾 This one is for real trivia buffs or maybe some random science types. Identify the two elements named after a small town in Sweden. Hint—their symbols are "Y" and "Yb". Give up? They are Ytterbium and Yttrium named for Ytterby, Sweden.

🐾 Here's a dreadful "Tom Swifty," "Frankly, my dear, I don't give a damn," said Tom rhetorically.

🐾 Scratch that old saying "It's darkest just before the dawn." It's actually darkest about 2 a.m. in the morning.

🐾 Going to write the President and give him a piece of your mind? On a normal day the President of the United States will receive your letter and about 20,000 others.

You Can Go Home Again If Only in Your Mind

❧ Thomas Wolfe wrote "You Can't Go Home Again" in 1940 and We Five sang "I Can Never go Home Again" in 1965, but they're both wrong. I did it not long ago. My mother's clan, the Iverson family, settled in eastern South Dakota in the 1860s and has gathered the extended family every Fourth of July for more than 80 years. The assemblage is typically at Iverson Park, a wooded tract of land along the Big Sioux River. The bluffs enclose the open glade and the river forms the backdrop. Food and fireworks are always on the menu, and conversation frequently turns nostalgic as family members no longer present are recalled.

I tested Wolfe's hypothesis by running from my Uncle Norm's farm down country lanes to the park, a distance of about 3½ miles. I found running against memories is like running against the wind. They buffet your face and tug at your legs so speed isn't an issue and your mind tends to wander back along those same roads. The distance in the 1940s was formidable, but today took just a little over half an hour to cover.

We Five and Wolfe were right about one thing. When you go back the size of most things is not as great as your mind recalls. The meals are good but not as tasty as your mind would say of those hot dogs and fried chickens of long ago. The only thing that hasn't changed is the love. Families mean love.

🐚 A century ago, 85 percent of U.S. workers were involved in agriculture. Today agriculture comprises less than three percent of the workforce. Few housewives can fruits and vegetables to prepare for the onslaught of winter. It's too easy to order a pizza.

🐚 Perhaps it explains why they're endangered. The only vegetarian marine mammals are the manatee and the dugong, both are native to the Americas.

🐚 You could say he had a nose for numbers. Tycho Brahe, a famous astronomer once challenged a fellow student to a sword fight to determine who was the best mathematician. He lost a chunk from his nose and wore a gold and silver replacement for years. I personally preferred the speed contests we held on the blackboards in Algebra. I retired undefeated with nose intact.

🐚 I guess it's all a matter of perspective. When Patrick Henry said, "Give me liberty or give me death" in 1775 he owned 65 slaves.

🐚 It doesn't matter to me. I couldn't hit it with help, but maybe some of you can. An international agreement in 1939 established 440 cycles per second for concert pitch A above middle C.

• Earl Wilson exhibited a nasty sense of humor when he said, "Women's liberation will not be achieved until a woman can become paunchy and bald and still think she's attractive to the opposite sex."

• Sorry to burst your bubble. The reason that puppies lick your face isn't that they're really affectionate and they love you. The puppies are just instinctively searching for bits of food.

• Here's a chance for those of you who like to try and catch me. The longest commonly used word in the English language with no letter appearing more than once is ambidextrously, 14 letters.

• Give me an "I," give me an "N," give me a "J." Each year, in the neighborhood of 16,000 cheerleaders in the United States seek emergency room treatment for cheerleader-related injuries.

• Parmesan cheese began its life in the Italian town of Parma where it was known as *parmigiano*.

• Had a metallurgical analysis performed recently? Tests have shown that intelligent people have more zinc and copper in their hair. I don't believe that this automatically condemns those who are "follicle-ly challenged" to stupidity.

• There's probably more than one message tucked away in this statistic. Alaska is the state with the highest percentage of folks who walk (snowshoe?) to work.

"What the Sam Hill?"

🐚 I don't know what all the fuss about Sam Hill was ("What the Sam Hill?"). James Hill was the man who should have been recognized. He came to St. Paul, Minnesota in 1856 as a 17-year-old shipping clerk. Within 22 years, he and some other investors bought the nearly bankrupt St. Paul and Pacific Railroad and pushed it west to the Pacific Ocean as the Great Northern Railway. Hill's personal influence allowed him to foster progress in agriculture and transportation for more than 30 years in the Northwest states. He called the railway the "great adventure" of his life and said, "When we are all dead and gone, the sun will shine, the rain will fall and the railroad will run as usual." His mansion in St. Paul is open to the public (maintained by the Minnesota Historical Society).

🐚 In case you were wondering, according to Dr. Fielding of the Edinburgh School of Agriculture, the number of horses world-wide exceeds 65 million. The number of donkeys (four-legged) is about 42 million, and mules come in at 15.5 million.

🐚 Lana Turner once said, "A successful man is one who makes more than his wife can spend—and a successful woman is one who can find such a man." Equal opportunity makes the flip side a challenge for today's single man.

• "Yes, Virginia, there is a Santa Claus" school. Actually there are several. The first one opened in Albion, New York on September 27, 1937. Apparently the cafeteria serves mostly carbohydrates in the form of pasta and potatoes.

• Being inducted into a hall of fame can be quite an honor. Unless it's the Dull Men's Hall of Fame as established by the Carroll, Iowa Chamber of Commerce. First inductees were Ozzie Nelson, Robert Young and Nigel Bruce. Spare me from ever being considered.

• I don't know who keeps this kind of record or who would perform the measurement, but the largest cockroach on record measures 3.81 inches.

• If I ever had a tombstone epitaph, I'd prefer this one. "He was born with a gift of laughter and a sense that the world was mad." The words were used once before, by Rafael Sabatini on his tombstone in Adelboden, Switzerland. Sabatini wrote the words to describe the hero of his 1921 novel, *Scaramouche*. The novel became a fine '50s film starring Stewart Granger.

• I don't think I can add anything to this one. Steven Spielberg named the large mechanical shark used in *Jaws*, Bruce, after his lawyer.

• I know you're probably guessing the oldest American College sport is beer drinking, but it's not, it's rowing. The former is sport but not a sport.

❧ Call 'em as you see 'em. That rock band, Dire Straits, took its name from a friend who was concerned about the band's finances. No reference was implied about their music.

❧ If you were around before 1926 (and paying attention) you might remember that no one ever said, "hitchhike." The term was coined that year.

❧ How about a "toast" to the toaster. The first electric toaster of the type we're all used to was marketed in June 1926 by the McGraw Electric Company under the trademark, "Toastmaster." The nifty little device could do one slice at a time (no bagels) and cost $13.50.

❧ You can't make footprints in the sands of time sitting down, so think about what impression you want to leave.

❧ Been there, done that (in a prior life). More than half of us Americans get out of bed before 7:00 a.m. local time.

❧ My personal efforts are either leading the league of "griffonage" or are close to it. "Griffonage" is the term used to describe illegible handwriting. Maybe I should have been a doctor?

❧ Under the category of home remedies, or at least ancient Chinese home remedies: They used to swing their arms to cure a headache. Let me know how it works for you. I take buffered aspirin.

Not Really
A Very Dry Martini

🍸 The cotton gin was not just another form of really dry martini. When Eli Whitney invented his mechanical cotton picker in 1792 he did not choose the name "cotton gin" out of his deference to a particular alcoholic beverage. Whitney wasn't even from the South. He first named it "cotton engine" then shortened it to cotton gin because he believed that was a more attractive term for southern cotton farmers.

The cotton gin significantly changed the economy in the South but did little in Whitney's benefit. His machine was so simple and efficient that almost any proficient mechanic could copy it so by 1797 his company was out of business.

🍸 I know the rim size varied night to night for me. Hard to believe as it is, the diameter of a basketball rim is more than twice the diameter of the ball: 19 inches for the rim, and just slightly more than 9 inches for the ball. The nights the rim seemed to be 27 inches were the most fun.

❧ The 1970s were really a weird time in music history. Disco flourished to the extent that "Disco Duck" a novelty song by Rick Dees and his Cast of Idiots actually hit Number One. Some good sense prevailed however, and his tribute to the new *King Kong* movie, "Dis-Gorilla" died on the vine.

❧ You know how the Los Angeles Dodgers got their name. The Brooklyn Dodgers moved west. The question is "How did the Brooklyn Dodgers get their name?" The fast moving and numerous New York streetcars created enough concern among the residents that they called themselves trolley dodgers. When the team got its start in the late 1800s it was natural to call their team the Dodgers.

❧ Polka dots is a term that earned its name. The dotted fabric became extremely popular as a dress material at the time the polka craze was peaking.

❧ Ivan the Terrible couldn't have been too terrible; he was married seven times. He must have had that desperate charm some of us possess.

❧ Flexing them a side at a time is really tricky. You have nine muscles in each ear if you're a normal human. Some people can wiggle them intriguingly.

❧ Many of us know of what Ogden Nash spoke when he commented, "Middle age is when you've met so many people that every new person you meet reminds you of someone else."

❧ Pay attention, the "prez" is coming. James K. Polk, the 11th president was so undistinguished in appearance that his wife Sarah arranged for the Marine Band to play "Hail to the Chief," an old Scottish anthem whenever he entered the room. It became tradition in 1845 and is still today.

❧ Timing is everything. In the 13th century many Europeans baptized children with beer.

❧ What, me worry! People ages 24 to 35 on the average worry less than adults in any other age group.

❧ I can't remember if I've printed this quote from Steven Wright. "Right now, I'm having amnesia and de'ja vu at the same time. I think I've forgotten this before."

❧ Do you know why some kids are fussier eaters than adults? I was and maybe this explains it. Children have more taste buds than adults do.

❧ Hydrangeas are the opposite of litmus. Well, not exactly, but they behave the opposite of a litmus test. Litmus, a dye developed from lichen, turns pink if dipped in an acid, and blue if exposed to an alkali (surely you remember that from Chemistry). Hydrangeas tend to grow pink in alkaline soil and blue in acid soil. It does take longer to test the soil using these flowers than using a litmus test.

❧ I'll bet you won't remember this word for long: lethologica. It means the inability to remember a word.

Hats off to J.B.

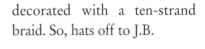

&. If John Batterson Stetson hadn't been in poor health, who knows how long it might have taken? Stetson went west at the time of the Civil War and noticed that no one was manufacturing hats suited to the practical needs of the cowboy. He returned to Philadelphia in the mid-1860s and started a hat business specializing in western-style headgear. The wide-brimmed hats he designed immediately became popular with cowboys and remain so today. That "ten gallon" thing doesn't relate to the capacity (it's closer to ten pints). It came from the Americanization of the Spanish word for braid *galón*. The early hats were decorated with a ten-strand braid. So, hats off to J.B.

&. Bruno Colapietro, a matrimonial lawyer, offers this bit of learned wisdom, "When women marry, they think their husbands will change. When men marry, they think their wives will never change. Both are wrong." A few exceptions exist, these couples celebrate ruby, sapphire and gold anniversaries.

&. I'm not allowed to do personal research on this one, but my references tell me Kanebo Ltd., a Japanese company, manufactures and markets a line of women's pantyhose embossed with tiny capsules of seaweed fibers, vitamins and other nutrients. These capsules break on contact with the skin, and the contents are absorbed, yielding smoother, healthier (nicer-looking) legs.

🐾 It's good, but it's not as good as Marionberry Cobbler. The official state dessert of Massachusetts is Boston Cream Pie.

🐾 I'd turn down a scholarship offer if I were you. The California Academy of Tauromaquia in San Diego teaches bull-fighting.

🐾 At least it was one of the early instances of equal opportunity. The diet of that mythical monster, the Minotaur, periodically included seven youths and seven maidens.

🐾 Let me augment your level of sophis-tication by defining these two terms used in the making of champagne. *Crus* refers to the different wines to be used in the blend. *Cuv'ee* to the actual blending. Now when you order the bubbly you can speak (or read the menu) knowledgeably.

🐾 You get the sense Prime Minister Winston Churchill thought his successor, Clement Attlee, was a "wuss" when he described him as "a sheep in sheep's clothing."

🐾 There are several comments I could make here, but you'll have to guess at them or come up with your own. Nauru, an island in the Pacific, has an economy built almost entirely on bird droppings.

❧ He may have had more to do with the taming of the West than Samuel Colt. John Deere invented the first practical steel plow, which cut through black prairie soil much better than the iron plows in use. His 1837 invention was the building block on which John Deere became the largest agricultural machinery manufacturer in the world.

❧ In summer months in mosquito territory, hang around with blond children. Mosquitoes are more attracted to children than they are to adults and prefer blondes to brunettes.

❧ Know anybody like this? Roughly one fourth of the people attending sporting events think their presence affects the outcome of the game.

❧ There's a lot of truth in this line from the King, "I don't know anything about music. In my line (of work) you don't have to." Elvis Presley (1935–1977).

❧ If "an apple a day keeps the doctor away," how many physician-free days does 8,284 apples generate? That's how many you eat in a lifetime if you're an average American. Of those, almost half are Red Delicious while sadly only about 316 are Jonathans.

❧ The single river that touches more countries than any other is the Danube. On its journey from Germany to the Ukraine it contacts or borders ten countries in Europe. It's also one of the few rivers to have its own waltz; others being the Tennessee and the Missouri.

Sodas Aren't Just for Jerks

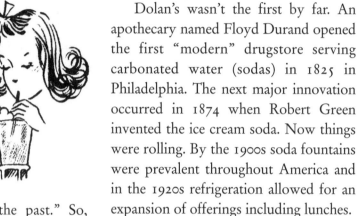

❧ Friends provide me motivation and ideas. At a recent retirement party one came up to me and said "I like your column; you make me remember things from the past." So, Connie, this one's for you.

Soda fountains were the greatest places to gather as teenagers in those kinder, gentler days of yore. I particularly remember Dolan's in my hometown. Dolan was also the freshman football coach so he may have had a secondary purpose in fattening up the skinny teenagers who frequented his establishment.

Dolan's wasn't the first by far. An apothecary named Floyd Durand opened the first "modern" drugstore serving carbonated water (sodas) in 1825 in Philadelphia. The next major innovation occurred in 1874 when Robert Green invented the ice cream soda. Now things were rolling. By the 1900s soda fountains were prevalent throughout America and in the 1920s refrigeration allowed for an expansion of offerings including lunches.

I think the industry peaked in the early 1940s and then soda jerks—so called because they "jerked" the fountain handles forward to draw soda water into a glass—were drafted, sugar was rationed, and the war changed our lives.

Soda fountains have never really come back; they've been replaced by miscellaneous "fast-foodery." However, an occasional small town or resort area may have a reconstruction, and they're well worth patronizing, even if you can watch your shake or malt go directly to a part of your anatomy where it never did as a kid.

🐾 I offer the "Things That Bite Rule" from a California biogeographer. "As a matter of biology, not sexism, if something bites you, it's probably female."

🐾 The Number One record for the first three decades of the Rock and Roll era (1955–1984) was Elvis Presley's double-sided 45 rpm hit, "Hound Dog / Don't Be Cruel." Got it in the original version in my library of oldies and goodies.

🐾 Think about applying Murphy's Law to Newton's Law of gravity. You still have "What goes up must come down," but

now don't expect it to land where you can find it.

🐾 Most readers would know that the St. Louis Rams moved from L.A. to St. Louis, but how many knew that the franchise began as the Cleveland Rams? When the franchise was founded in 1937 the management resisted the push to name the team similar to the baseball team, the Indians. Instead, the team was named the Rams after a college team, the Fordham Rams. In 1945, the Rams became the first NFL franchise to switch cities with their move to Los Angeles.

🐾 And speaking of switching cities, if you can't come up with airfare to Athens, Greece you can always drive to Nashville, Tennessee and see a full-scale, clean version of the Parthenon. Sure, it's not the same, but Nashville is cleaner and less polluted than Athens.

⁊ Enjoy your time at the beach? There are a lot of opportunities. Earth has more than 300,000 miles of coastlines.

⁊ I've certainly used her name at times, but I don't ever think I've taken it in vain. Belinda Blurb was a model who was portrayed on a book jacket by illustrator Gelett Burgess. Belinda's name inspired the term used for a publisher's comments on a book cover (or any other brief commentary, a "blurb").

⁊ Is it the cosmopolitan life style and dining choices, or is it the absence of natural hazards? The average city dog lives about three years longer than his rural counterpart. That bodes well for Twoey.

⁊ Thank goodness I've not been afflicted with Graphophobia. It's the fear of writing in public.

⁊ I like this thought by John Homer Miller: "Your living is determined not so much by what life brings to you as by the attitude you bring to life."

⁊ Norman Rockwell painted more than 300 *Saturday Evening Post* covers. Many of us saw Americana through his eyes and brush.

⁊ They had a good run, but nothing lasts forever. The manufacture of 78 rpm records was discontinued in 1958. The major culprit was the little 45 rpm record.

CRASH

It was great sport to drive my train right through the fort. Lest you think I was a psychopathic railway engineer in an early life, let me clarify. It was an electric train, and I'd built the fort of Lincoln Logs. Like many young boys in the 1940s and early '50s I had a great set of Lincoln Logs with which I could build frontier stuff. Only recently did I realize that those building toys had a real architectural background. John Lloyd, the son of well-known architect Frank Lloyd Wright, invented the logs. You'd think they'd have traded on the family name and called them Lloyd Logs instead of using Abe's fabled youth.

Count 'em yourself or find a curious friend. Keeping track is what's tough. Most people have at least twenty-five moles (on their bodies).

Some folk songs have a historical basis in fact. Laura Foster was the young woman murdered by Tom Dula. Sheriff Jim Grayson subsequently arrested Dula. The Kingston Trio immortalized the entire unfortunate event in their 1958 Number One Hit, "Tom Dooley." The original folk song was written in 1866 as "Tom Dula."

I'll bet your daughter or granddaughter isn't included in the one percent of teenage American girls who doesn't use a deodorant.

The "Spam Caper" just won't go away. I've recently discovered that there is a SPAM Museum in Austin, Minnesota located at 1937 SPAM Boulevard (SPAM was invented in 1937). There is a 12-minute film on the product's history as well as a puppet show explaining how SPAM got started. You can buy SPAM T-shirts and other memorabilia, but bring your favorite SPAMwich for lunch, there is no cafeteria. By the way, Hormel sells more than 122 million cans of SPAM around the world every year.

Having a tough day and feeling really low? It could be worse. You could be having that day in the Maldives. The 19 clusters of coral atolls (islands) that make up the Maldives have a maximum elevation of eight feet above sea level. Most of the country lies very close to sea level making it the country to have the lowest maximum elevation in the world. The Maldives became independent from British protection in 1965.

Milton Berle once suggested: "You know you're getting old when you're sitting in a rocker, and you can't get it started."

It's a mark for us aging runners to shoot at. In 1969, Larry Lewis ran the 100-yard dash in 17.8 seconds. Not a blur you say, but Lewis was 101 years old and set a new record in the 100-years-or-older class.

I don't know about you but I'm not reorganizing my library. "Lady Gough's Book of Etiquette" from Victorian days notes that arranging books so that a book written by a male author placed by a book written by a female author to which he is not married is simply not done. Maybe she was worried about them having illegitimate short stories.

🐦 You could see how this literary morality thing could easily get out of hand. In the Sears Roebuck catalog of 1962 not one woman modeling Sears maternity lingerie wore a wedding ring.

🐦 Most of us use his invention two to three times a day. Dentist Dr. Washington Wentworth Sheffield invented the toothpaste tube in 1892. He developed a flexible, collapsible metal tube that replaced the porcelain jars then in use. You can't squeeze a jar to get the last brushful out.

🐦 Recall the name of the last of the Alabammus Hammus breed of pig? Sure, it was Salomey, Little Abner's pig in Al Capp's comic strip.

🐦 Want to feel bad? At the age of four, Andre Agassi hit tennis balls for 15 minutes with Jimmy Connors, winner of the most tennis tournaments is history. Glad I didn't play him at age four.

🐦 I'd guess you know a baby kangaroo is called a "joey." What's your guess on what its parents are called? "Mom and Dad" is a nice try, but Down Under the mother is a "flyer" and the father a "boomer."

🐦 Got a couple of rowdy friends? Watch it! The minimum number of people necessary for a disturbance to be called a riot is three, according to criminal law.

Out of Your Mind? Which Mind?

🌿 If someone says to you, "You're not in your right mind" it might be good depending on what you're doing. For right-handers—and perhaps 90 percent of us fall in this category—the left side of our brain controls skills like reading, writing and talking and is responsible for most of our logic and analytical thinking. The right side of our brain is mostly involved with creativity, imagination and feelings.

So if you're balancing your checkbook, preparing a report or analyzing a proposal "not being in your right mind"

might be just fine. Most left-handers are similar to right-handed people, but not all are. In the case of those folks the functions are reversed.

Now if you want to activate your creative side, you can listen to music from the Baroque Period, and it will help free your right brain for new thoughts or ideas. For me, I listen to music from my "broke period" (the '50s) and it seems to help me. Solitary physical activity like running, biking and walking can also provide endorphins that stimulate your thinking. Just a note—sometimes when you hear that you're not in your right mind it's a warning that the tight-fitting white jacket is coming.

❧ Sometimes I almost hate myself. Did you hear about the female plumber named Molly who lived in Denver? She invented a stainless steel kitchen sink. Naturally she named it the "Unbrownable Molly Sink."

❧ The ancient Incas measured time by how long it took a potato to cook. Maybe their descendents are now measuring time by the speed of French fries at a fast food restaurant.

❧ It's a good thing we don't pay them mileage. Red blood cells typically live around four months during which time they may make 75,000 round trips to the lungs and back.

❧ What a difference a half-century makes! In the early 1950s only one in every 14 women dyed her hair. Today it's three out of every four and may still include that woman from the '50s.

❧ Feeling low on your B-vitamin intake? Stand out in the rain awhile (if you can find it). Rain contains vitamin B12.

❧ Perhaps you saw her Emmy award-winning performance. Jackie Kennedy was awarded a special Emmy for her conducted tour of the White House on television. She did the tour to prod Congress into passing legislation that would give the White House status as a permanent museum. She was the only First Lady to receive an Emmy.

❧ I can't be certain, but this may give an indication of what's going on with the stock market. Roughly three of every ten

American men say the unstable economy is responsible for their watching more cartoons on television.

❧ This Japanese proverb is brief, to the point and I'm afraid oh so true. "No medicine cures stupidity."

❧ Be sure to time your next lunar eclipse. One should last no longer than seven minutes and 58 seconds. Any longer and you may be suffering a personal eclipse.

❧ Yeah, sure! The words that are most used in U.S. television ads are "new" and "improved." That doesn't cut it for a number of us who liked some things the way they were.

❧ Many of us more senior citizens remember Frederick Schiller Faust much better by his pen name, Max Brand. Max—or Fred—was the creator of *Dr. Kildare* and writer of *Destry Rides Again.*

❧ The colors of the five Olympic rings are blue, red, yellow, black and green. There's a reason. At least one of those colors appears in the flag of every nation in the world. It's a wonder Lifesavers hasn't come up with a matching tube.

❧ Radio newscaster Gabriel Heatter's tag line has certainly gone by the wayside in today's delight in disaster broadcasts. Heatter began with "Ah, there's good news tonight."

A Little Learning Goes
A Long Way

❧ I remember the names of mine and you probably remember the names of yours, too. I'm referring to those teachers who impacted our lives. Eileen Cline started me out right in kindergarten. Miss Helland not only put up with me as a student teacher, she taught me all of the math through Trigonometry. Guy O. Karnes (you never called him "Guy O." to his face) was Teacher of the Year in both South Dakota and Minnesota. And Miss Malmstrom liked my New Mexico accent for Spanish better than her Swedish one.

Although it may have seemed like it to me, none of them graduated from the very first teacher training school in the

United States established at Concord, Vermont in 1823. I never thanked them properly at the time, and now it's too late. Don't let that happen to any of yours if you still have the opportunity.

❧ If you were to "look a gift horse in the mouth," you could determine its sex. Male horses typically have 40 teeth while females possess 36.

❧ My Grandma Willard and Henny Youngman's could have played cards at the same table. He said of her, "My grandmother is over 80 and still doesn't need glasses. Drinks right out of the bottle."

❧ Can you guess the three weapons allowed in the sport of fencing? They are the foil, epee' and saber. Scratch that guess of picket.

❧ I like quirky little shop names. I had coffee not long ago in Portland at a funky little place named "Rimsky Korsakoffee." The background music was classical, as were the desserts. You might recall Rimsky Korsakov's "Flight of the Bumblebee" as the theme for the TV series, "The Green Hornet." The late Al Hirt performed it.

❧ He probably qualified for worker's compensation. During the filming of the 1967 movie *Dr. Dolittle*, Rex Harrison was bitten by a parrot, a dog, a chimp and a duck. The script did not call for it. The animals were overacting.

❧ That thought-provoking challenge that frequently shares the section space with columns like this, the crossword puzzle was first developed by Arthur Wynne in 1913. The "New York World" published the first version in its Sunday Supplement on December 21.

❧ The winter season sees twice as many heart attacks as summer does. Why spoil a good tan?

❧ The rock group UB40 fittingly took their name from the designation of the British unemployment benefit form.

❧ I always thought cutting onions was just sad work until I ran onto this. When you cut an onion the pierced cells release a sulfur compound (thio-propanal-s-oxide), through a series of speedy chemical reactions. It is this substance that is irritating to the eyes.

❧ A MADAM isn't what you think it is. This MADAM is different from a madam you might be more familiar with. MADAM (Manchester automatic digital machine) was a chess-playing machine designed by Alan Turing in 1950. He was one of the first individuals to program a computer to play chess. Unfortunately his device was a poor chess player and made foolish moves. After several such moves the machine would be forced to give up. No mention is made of whether the machine was a good loser or not.

❧ He's probably not working for tips anymore. Rob Angel is the Seattle waiter who invented the game Pictionary in 1986.

❧ The nickname might fit quite a few of us in society today. Baseball Hall of Famer Luke Appling was known as "Old Aches and Pains" because of his frequent injuries.

The Chicken, the Egg, the Mouse, the Cat?

🐾 Which came first, the mouse or the cat? Actually it was the cat. Felix the Cat was the first cartoon superstar. He appeared in a short called "Feline Follies" (a silent film) in 1919, and it was so popular that Pat Sullivan's production studio produced 26 cartoons a year. Felix was such a hit he was the New York Yankees' lucky mascot in 1922, shared the screen with Charlie Chaplin in 1923 and a Felix doll accompanied Lindbergh in 1927 on his Trans-Atlantic flight. Alas, when "talkies" came out Sullivan didn't pick up on them, and Felix' popularity waned. He did appear in the comics from 1923–1967 and then again from 1984–1987 but more people remember Mickey.

🐾 On the average, rabbits take about 18 naps a day. I wonder what makes them so tired.

🐾 I think we should take serious note of this quote from Gloria Steinem, "One day, an army of gray-haired women may quietly take over the earth." I'll tell you what bothers me. They may be having organizational meetings in my house.

&. This may explain the behavior of some people. The planet Earth is 0.02 degrees hotter during a full moon.

&. Who'd want to invade? Iceland has no standing army.

&. Many cheeses are named after the place of their origin. Gouda is a compressed sphere of cheese named for the Dutch town of Gouda. Colby cheese was first made in Colby, Wisconsin at the close of the 19th century. Monterey Jack was created by David Jacks in Monterey, California at about the same time. Colby Jack must have been the result of a clandestine meeting in Denver.

&. Puzzle fans may see these as a challenge. I see them as an opportunity to recycle. I'm talking about the new jigsaw puzzles called "Impossibles." They are 750-piece jigsaw puzzles with edge pieces that look like inner pieces and five extra pieces that don't belong in the puzzle. It's possible that psychiatrists with a shortage of patients devised these nasty little pastimes.

&. Most housecats can sprint as fast as 30 miles per hour for short distances (although they have to do it of their own volition).

&. The expression that something "fits to a 'T'" comes from the idea that it fits as well as if it was constructed using an engineer's T-square. I guess that's OK if you want clothes designed by an engineer. My experience is that most of them are not epitomes of sartorial elegance.

❦ Lita Chaplin, Charlie Chaplin's ex-wife, stated Charlie's genius was in comedy; he had no sense of humor. I'd guess a lot of ex-wives would describe their prior husbands in the same way.

❦ Margarine has an interesting history. It was invented in 1869 as a butter substitute for use during shortages in the wars of Napoleon III. The ingredients were beef fat and margaric acid. When it emigrated to the U.S. it ran into opposition from dairy farmers, and Congress passed the Margarine Act in 1886. Legislation remained in place through World War II and most families who couldn't get butter, or afford the high-priced (by taxes) colored margarine had to buy white margarine and color it themselves (many of us remember that). Federal restrictions were finally lifted in 1950, and Wisconsin was the last state to drop its ban on coloring.

❦ Step through this one by Emo Phillips, "I used to think that the human brain was the most fascinating part of the body, and then I realized, 'What is telling me that?'"

❦ Mort Sahl who possessed a nasty sense of humor once queried, "There are two politicians drowning and you are allowed to save only one. What do you do? Read a newspaper or eat your lunch?"

❦ Maybe it's the reason I don't listen to talk shows. You hear about 11,000 words spoken in every hour on the radio.

Sweets for the Sweet?

❧ The subject of chocolate has surfaced again. A dear friend gave us truffles for Christmas (no, he didn't snuffle out that kind, he bought these at a candy shop).

I've flirted with chocolate over the years. I used to keep a cache of Brach's chocolate stars for rewards when I finished my math homework in high school.

Richard Cadbury—still a name in chocolate—introduced the first box of chocolates to England in 1868, and it's been all down hill ever since. Americans spend about $1 billion on chocolate candy every Valentine's Day. The French go us one better. The Yacht Club of France recently celebrated the 20th anniversary of the *Club des Croqeurs de Chocolat* (basically Chocoholics Anonymous of France) as twenty of the finest patisseries served chocolate desserts.

I wasn't there; it's very difficult to obtain invitations. You and I will simply have to satisfy ourselves with whatever the local guilt will allow.

❧ In what I hope is an unrelated item, Rhesus monkeys fed a typical American diet in labs died within two years.

❧ Many of us struggle with reality. Ferdinand I, the emperor of Austria in the 1800s was probably struggling more than most of us. The most coherent sentence he spoke during his reign was, "I am the emperor, and I want dumplings." Personally, I'd have asked for popcorn.

🐾 If you had read every book (no specials) you'd have read over 900 books by now. The Book-of-the-Month Club was established in New York City in April of 1926. The first selection was "Lolly Willowes; Or the Loving Huntsman." No, I'm not reviewing it.

🐾 Just in case you happen to be in the neighborhood, be aware (or beware) the Trapshooting Hall of Fame is located in Vandalia, Ohio. I'm kind of curious about the exhibits: used clay pigeons?

🐾 Will Rogers said this quite a while ago, but I suspect the truth has survived the years and perhaps flourished. "Let advertisers spend the same amount of money improving their product that they do advertising, and they wouldn't have to advertise it."

🐾 I might forgive them Anne but not the dog. When the Brits beheaded Anne Boleyn (another of Henry's also-rans) they also beheaded her wolfhound.

🐾 Something you might consider the next time you're buying that frilly something for a gift or for yourself, the word negligee is derived from the Latin *neglegere* which means to neglect (implying housework).

🐾 And be sure to bring back the receipts. Congress alloted Meriwether Lewis and William Clark the sum of $2,500 to cover their trip expenses from May 1804 through September 1806. I don't see the problem. I didn't spend that much when I retraced their route almost 200 years later. Of course, many of the tribes they traded with didn't take plastic.

❧ More senior readers might recall the first "career girl" comic strip. Martin Branner's "Winnie Winkle" appeared on the scene in 1920, years before that situation was commonplace.

❧ In the sport of archery, that term a "Robin Hood" does not mean nailing a sheriff wandering too close to the forest. A "Robin Hood" occurs when the tip and shaft of a subsequent arrow fired at the target is shot deep into an arrow already in the bull's eye.

❧ I can't help but agree with George Mitchell's viewpoint, "Although He is regularly asked to do so, God does not take sides in American politics."

❧ No wonder most of the critters up there look pale; there's no tanning season.

The North Pole sees no sun for 186 days during each year.

❧ This is about the worst thing you can call any level of government. Try "Kakistocracy." The word means government of a state by its worst citizens.

❧ This palindrome is particularly appropriate at tax time. "No, I save on final perusal, a sure plan if no evasion."

❧ If they'd only had a better press agent we might now be living in Pinzona! Martin Alonzo Pinzon and his brother Vicente Yanez Pinzon captained the Pinta and the Nina while Chris was on the Santa Maria in 1492.

Twenty Questions, Twenty Answers?

🌶 Animal, vegetable or mineral? "20 Questions" was a great game to play while traveling with our kids. It postponed the "Are we there yet?" questions for a few moments. The game was one of those great old radio shows. It aired on the Mutual Broadcasting Network from 1946 through 1954. The emcee worked with a panel of four or five and the listening audience who tried to outguess the panelists.

The proliferation of TV game shows finished it off since it was a game played in the mind and intellectual stimulation isn't TV's forte. The size of the breadbox was a known item at that time.

🌶 The fabrics really only look brighter. Those fabric brighteners are in fact "optical bleaches" that act by reflecting blue light. The blue light combines with the yellow discoloration in the fabric to produce white light that makes the cloth seem brighter. I don't know how you feel about that, but I'm still convinced my T-shirts have a very finite life span.

🌶 The Lone Ranger never smoked. Nor did most of the old cowboy heroes. It wasn't much of a reason but that (and athletics) kept me from trying it. Today, I'm glad. The risk that a first-time user will become addicted to cigarettes is nine in ten, odds I wouldn't want to bet.

❧ Like to impress your friends and acquaintances with unusual words in conversation? Try "wallydrag." Just be careful how you use it. It means a completely useless person.

❧ That term "put a sock in it" dates to the early days of Victrolas. The first products were hand-wound with no volume control. Listeners soon discovered you could lower the volume by literally putting a sock in the phonograph's horn.

❧ The "bestseller" lists for 1887 aren't available anymore, but if they were they might reflect *A Study in Scarlet.* Sir Arthur Conan Doyle introduced one of histories all-time greatest detectives in that work.

❧ A tall shortstop sounds like a real oxymoron. Cal Ripken at six feet four inches holds the major league height record for that position.

❧ I've never shot an eagle or a birdie, par is extremely rare, bogies rare but random. I have shot a snowman on a number of occasions when it wasn't snowing on the course. A snowman? That's when you shoot an "8" on a hole (notice the physical similarity?). I guess it's also when you shoot "88" on a round, but I wouldn't know.

❧ This knowledge puts a whole new perspective on my orders in Italian restaurants. The literal translation of that pasta known as *vermicelli* is "little worms."

❧ You might consider him a real "home boy." Stephen Foster had two of his compositions adopted as official state anthems. Kentucky chose "My Old Kentucky Home," and Florida naturally selected "Old Folks at Home."

❧ I have a great deal in common with Richard Diran who said, "I have a rock garden. Last week three of them died."

❧ Only two presidents of the United States have been bald, John Quincy Adams and Dwight Eisenhower. The physical qualifications must be similar to those for TV news anchors.

❧ Got any addictions? I can claim running, but running pales in comparison to some critters I know. These little junkies are yellow-bellied marmots. They hang out in little marmot gangs in the Mineral King area of Sequoia National Park in California and wait for unsuspecting motorists to park their cars. No, they don't jump out and mug them. They surreptitiously sneak up under the hoods of automobiles and quaff antifreeze to their heart's (or liver's) content. The nasty sweet flavor and aroma can be fatal to dogs, cats and humans, but the marmots just seem to get a bit of a "high." Some of these little "dopers" have traveled under the car hoods as far as Seattle to feed their habit. Frequently, tagged addict marmots are moved miles away only to return. I suppose the next step for them is smoking.

Baby, It's Cold Inside

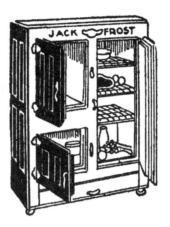

Many people still called it an icebox when I was a kid, but the origin of the refrigerator began with the discovery of the principles of artificial refrigeration in 1748 by Scottish scientist William Cullen at the University of Glasgow. Cullen evaporated ethyl ether into a partial vacuum heralding the dawn of vapor cooling.

Almost one hundred years passed before an American physician, John Gorrie, patented a refrigerator with a closed system and a compressor that was never marketed.

The first commercial home refrigerator, the Domelre, was available in 1913, and the icebox sales began to melt away (that method of food preservation dated to Ancient Greece). Kelvinator, General Electric and Frigidaire made the refrigerator one of the household necessities in the period between the two world wars.

It sounds like a nasty bit of improvised surgery. "Pierce my heart with a dull languor," the second line from "Ode to Autumn," a poem by Verlaine, was a key phrase broadcast by the BBC during World War II to let the French Underground know the D-Day invasion of Normandy was a go. A "dull languor" brings to mind a slow, lingering melancholy with a bad end.

🐾 You wouldn't normally consider it a substitute for pajamas. Gabrielle "Coco" Chanel created Chanel No. 5 in 1920. The perfume was her first manufactured scent. Marilyn Monroe claimed that was all she wore to bed thus the pajama line.

🐾 Flying standby wasn't very satisfying. The first commercial air flight in the United States took place on January 1, 1914. The route was from Tampa Bay, Florida to St. Petersburg a distance of 22 miles. The service carried only one passenger at a time and lasted for just a few weeks. One of the positive aspects was that little luggage was lost setting an expectation for future passengers.

🐾 For those into very finite measurements please note a single grain of sand is typically 1,500 times larger than a grain of clay.

🐾 The Nez Perce said something about together time in this proverb. "Talk to your children while they are eating; what you say will stay even after you are gone."

🐾 Oh what a difference five days made. Five days after the Battle of Lexington in 1775, the colonies learned that the British parliament had voted to allow them to tax themselves and provide for their own administration and civil defense.

🐾 She probably had some thoughts about it that we can be glad she didn't share. "The Muppet Show" was banned from TV in Saudi Arabia because one of its stars (Miss Piggy) was a pig.

🎵 That's a lot of fish food. A goldfish can live up to 25 years in captivity. I suspect placing the bowl near a television set would cut into that timeframe significantly.

🎵 The most common hat size for men is 7 ¹/₈ (my size). The size numbers have significance. That's the diameter in inches of the hat cavity.

🎵 R.D. Clyde expressed my philosophy on home projects precisely when he said, "It's amazing how long it takes to complete something you're not working on."

🎵 Most folks thought genies didn't have them. Barbara Eden of "I Dream of Jeannie" was never allowed to show her navel during the five-year run of the show. She's probably watching TV today and chuckling about her censors in this century.

🎵 It's oh so true. The meaning of that delightful dessert, *tiramisu,* means "pick me up" in Italian.

🎵 Polyvinyl acetate is a name that sounds like a finish applied to a kitchen counter. Oh, if only. In reality it's the main ingredient in most chewing gums presently being manufactured,

🎵 We can thank Carey Williams for summing it up thusly, "Youth is that period when a young boy (or girl) knows everything but how to make a living."

Drive It, Don't Park It

🎵 I hear it some times when I'm driving friends home, and it fits. Maybe you get it from your passengers on occasion. The phrase is "Home, James." The expression dates back to the 17th century and was a common command of English nobility given to their private coachmen. It was frequently followed with "and don't spare the horses." My friends don't usually add that part since they know I drive sedately.

🎵 Gideon Sundback deserves a big thank you from virtually everyone in America today. His invention "Hookless No. 2" slide fastener got its breakthrough in 1923 when the B.F. Goodrich Company used it on a line of rubber galoshes and a salesman for the company called it the "zipper" because he can close and open it quickly (zip it).

🎵 Pop music history notes (and maybe you recall it) that Harry Belafonte's 1956

LP was the first record album to sell more than one million copies. The top cut was "The Banana Boat Song (Day-O)."

🎵 Are you one of those folks with a lot of files at work or at home or both? Statistically, once you file something there's a 98 percent chance you will never access it again.

🎵 An old folk remedy says to treat mosquito bites, rub them with vinegar, oil, butter, onion, garlic or lemon peel and then blow on them (sounds more like a marinade). Or you could spray them with Willard Water.

🎵 The typical horse actually provides more than one horsepower. True it doesn't seem right, but your average horse can produce about 24 horsepower. One horsepower is the power required to lift 33,000 pounds one foot in one minute. The 24 horsepower number is based on a horse weighing just over 1,300 pounds.

🎵 The Duke said it plain, "Life is tough, but it's tougher when you're stupid."

🎵 They probably wouldn't have voted for him anyway. Andrew Jackson was involved in more than 100 duels before he became president.

🎵 Here's one of those great questions from "Ask Me Another," my trivia book from 1938. "Tell, within ten of the correct figure, the number of chemical elements now known." The answer given is 89. Now, we know that all atomic numbers above 92 are man-made in "atom-smashers" and my *Time-Life* 1965 book on matter stops at 103 with Lawrencium. My latest reference shows Meitnerium, a German discovery, at 109. Science marches on.

🐝 The wide-open spaces aren't very wide-open for most of us. The average American spends 69 years and 11 months indoors and five years outdoors in a lifetime.

🐝 There were only 51 manufactured, and the story of its demise is clouded. The Tucker was the creation of Preston Tucker in 1948. Noted stylist Alex Tremulis designed the four door "torpedo" sedan. Its flat six engine was rear-mounted for weight distribution. There was a center headlight that pivoted in the same direction as the front wheels and a padded dash for safety. The car could do 60 mph in 10 seconds and had a top speed of 120. One of those 51 in excellent condition today would bring about $100,000 to a collector.

🐝 An old Japanese proverb states, "Children yoke parents to the past, present and future." As always, the "yokes on us."

🐝 Compare yours for size and grace. Those shoes that carried Fred Astaire so marvelously across many dance floors were size 10½. No wonder I couldn't do it; mine are 11½.

🐝 Now it seems incongruous. The duration from the concept of "minute rice" to its realization as a product took 18 years (1931–1949).

Legal Eagles or
Barrister Buzzards?

🐾 Lawyers seem to be in high visibility in the media these days. Television programs (and the reported news) are either sanctifying them or vilifying them. You just don't see a "Saint Vili," who might have the human foibles we all share. I count some lawyers among my friends; they seem to be a lot like me (maybe wealthier).

I suggest we can lay the responsibility for our perspective on lawyers squarely at the feet of Erle Stanley Gardner. Gardner created super legal eagle Mason in 1933 in "The Case of the Velvet Claws." Mason appeared in 82 full-length novels, on radio from 1943 to 1955 and on TV from 1957 through 1966 and again in 1973. The 3,000

episodes on radio (it ran five days a week) were part soap opera and part detective series. When Perry hit TV for 271 episodes the focus was on courtroom drama. Throughout that time Perry only lost one case, when his client withheld evidence. He subsequently discovered it and exonerated her. With all the focus on Perry, we lost sight of the fact that Hamilton (Ham) Burger lost 270 of 271 cases and still retained his job. We can only hope that if we need legal assistance in the courtroom our lawyers saw Perry as a role model not Ham.

❧ Let's get this straight. The word spatula has nothing to do with a cuspidor. Spatula is derived from the same Latin root as are spoon, sword, spade and oar. When you think about it that's a pretty good fit. You can lift and scoop with one. You can cut soft stuff and you can blend a mixture using it like an oar. I try to use one occasionally just as a lark (I'm dangerous with pointed tools).

❧ Enjoy your hot groats this morning? When you eat a bowl of oatmeal you are actually eating groats. The groat is the name of the edible portion of the oat plant. You get a groat by removing the hull from an oat kernel.

❧ A Norseman went down with the Andrea Doria in July of 1956. No, it wasn't one of my latter-day Viking relatives; it was an experimental automobile made for Chrysler by Ghia of Italy. The tab for the Norseman was $100,000.

❧ Being first must give a team an edge. The Cincinnati Red Stockings were the first professional baseball team. Their record in 1869 was 65 wins, no losses, one tie. The next year, they won 130 games in a row. Makes you wonder if they were playing the Washington Generals.

❧ "She tore my valentine in two," said Tom halfheartedly.

❧ Shame on you if you're a member of the group. More than one fourth of all readers of novels skip ahead to find out what will happen in a book before they finish it.

❧ I wish I'd thought of that. The reason that the most sought-after Cracker Jack prize is a ring is that many of them then double as engagement rings.

❧ RRRibbittt! Frenchmen (and women) eat about 200 million frogs each year.

❧ If you serve a white wine with a fish dinner, should you serve white grapes with sushi?

❧ Don't try this at home. If perchance you could drive your auto straight up into the air, you could reach outer space in about 60 minutes (but what would you do then?).

❧ Here's another of those gems from Gloria Steinem, "Women may be the one group that grows more radical with age." Couple that with the army of gray-haired women and we've got a force to reckon with.

❧ Things you might not have known include the fact that Dwight D. Eisenhower was an avid bridge player. One of the criteria for service on his staff during World War II was an officer's ability to play bridge.

Sunday Funnies

As soon as I could read and realized there was more to life than "Dick and Jane," I turned to the cartoons. The word cartoon is derived from the Italian "cartone" meaning pasteboard. The earliest magazine drawing considered a cartoon appeared in 1843 in the English "Punch, or the London Charivari." The first was a social comment drawing by John Leech entitled "Shadow and Substance" picturing some poverty-stricken Londoners at an exhibition looking with bewilderment at the portraits of some gorgeous notables. I never saw that one. My personal favorite comic strip was Walt Kelly's inimitable "Pogo."

The first football player to have his jersey retired was old "Number 77," better known to many as "The Galloping Ghost" Red Grange. In later years, my basketball teams kept retiring my number only to see me reappear (to their chagrin) wearing a different number.

❧ This is my kind of duel. When the French literary historian and critic Charles Augustin Sainte-Beuve was challenged to a duel by a journalist and offered his choice of weapons he said, "I choose spelling. You're dead."

❧ How did we get along before his invention? In 1937, Sylvan Goldman invented the shopping cart. At least then they weren't strewn throughout parking lots by lazy shoppers.

❧ Most of us remember Albert Einstein, few of us remember Adolf Fisch. Pity, had it not been for Fisch we wouldn't have known of Einstein. As a youth, he saved Einstein's life by grabbing his arm when Einstein slipped as they were climbing an 8,000-foot mountain.

❧ How did they do that? In the 1951 film, "Royal Wedding," Fred Astaire danced on the walls, the ceiling and occasionally on the floor of his hotel suite. In the pre-computer graphics era, the film used a set that rotated like a rotisserie. I'd have believed that Fred could do it without help.

❧ I don't think I want to watch. The Stampede and Suicide race is held in Omak, Washington in August. The event has horses and riders racing down a cliff and across a river.

❧ It certainly was a fitting gesture to an incredible man. In 1931, millions of Americans dimmed their lights for a few moments to salute the passing of Thomas Edison.

A Pipsisewah Is a Real Pip!

❧ What would a "Pipsisewah" look like to you? How about a "Skeezix"? Howard Garis knew what they looked like. Garis began his stories of Uncle Wiggily, the bunny rabbit gentleman, in the Evening News of Newark, New Jersey in the early years of the 20th century.

Whitman Publishing Company printed smaller illustrated versions of the stories in 1940 with the artwork done by Lang Campbell. Now interested children could see the Skeezix was a skinny crow-looking creature who walked on two legs and the Pipsisewah had a head like a rhinoceros and a bottom like a pudgy pig.

In addition to these enemies, Uncle Wiggily had friends like Jackie and Peetie Bow-Wow, the doggie boys and Jacko and Jumpo, the monkey boys. Nurse Jane Fuzzy Wuzzy, the muskrat lady housekeeper was his regular companion (I suppose they were living in sin, but I didn't give it much thought). Garis provided thousands of kids with delightful adventures of Uncle Wiggily which even children of today love (or so my grandkids would tell you).

❧ The "Wooden O" was what Shakespeare and his counterparts called it. The circular Globe Theater was built in 1598 and referred to in a chorus in "Henry V." The famous venue burned down in 1613 and was rebuilt in 1614.

That version of the theater lasted until 1644 when it was destroyed by the Puritans, who opposed entertainment.

🐾 In my mind he looked a lot older. Francisco Vazquez de Coronado was 30 years old when he discovered the Grand Canyon and introduced horse, mules, cattle, sheep and pigs to the American Southwest in 1540.

🐾 I'm a dog lover, but here's an intriguing observation from August Strindberg, "People who keep dogs are cowards who haven't got the guts to bite people themselves." I assume he was referring to burglars.

🐾 Are you an only child? Scratch the U.S. presidency from your list of career goals. All U.S. presidents have had at least one sibling (for better or worse).

🐾 "Where's the beef? Indeed. The standard precooked weight of a McDonald's hamburger is 1.6 ounces (other comparable brands are probably similar).

🐾 In a directly related item, the average number of sesame seeds on a Big Mac bun is 178. Order several, count them and take an average if you're having a slow day. Burpppp.

🐾 We're uncertain how effective he was as a general but Daniel Butterfield, a Union general during the U.S. Civil War, wrote the immortal music for "Taps."

❧ "Around the world in …" 83 days, 9 hours and 54 minutes? The U.S.S. Triton was the first submarine to go around the world submerged. You may recall it happened in 1960.

❧ I've still got a great scar from my childhood case of varicella, maybe you have one too. Varicella is the medical name for chicken pox. I guess chickenpox wasn't descriptive enough for medical usage.

❧ I suppose he'd be among the first to know. The late Adlai Stevenson defined a politician as "One who approaches every situation with an open mouth."

❧ Considering a backup career? Three out of every five burglars simply walk in to places they burgle. Only 40 percent actually have to break in to buildings.

❧ If you're male try this on your significant other. I love you for your "muliebrity." Before she hits you, hasten to explain "muliebrity" means the quality of being womanly, a softness, a feminity. It has nothing to do with mulishness or stubbornness.

❧ Modesto, California got its name because its founders were too modest to name it after themselves.

❧ There was a crispness to it for certain. The first motto inscribed on U.S. coins was "Mind your own business" in 1789.

ACKNOWLEDGMENTS

Publishing a book is not the ripening of the fruit from a vine planted by one person. There are a number of people to whom I am indebted for this little volume appearing in print. The first two names to come to mind are my fellow authors Greg Piburn and Ken Jessen. Both were extremely encouraging and helpful as I began the process.

This all began when Bob Rummel, the general manager of the *Loveland Daily Reporter-Herald*, took a chance that someone like me with little journalistic experience could write a regular column and make it interesting to readers. Bob, Rick Carpenter, and Jackie Hutchins (my editor) guided me along the learning curve. The *Longmont Times-Call* and the *Cañon City Daily Record* joined my group and today Val Baker and Lee Spaulding of those papers encourage my efforts.

My two daughters have been faithful readers and have helped catch me in questionable items and my son continues to provide me technical assistance. My wife, MJ, has put up with me being a trivial kind of guy for almost five decades. My parents, Myron and Esther, gave me the genes (and my jeans for 17 years) for a mind with a Velcro wall that had items stick to it. In the last couple years, Twoey, my Bichon frise-Maltese research associate, has been a constant companion who got me out of my chair from time to time to stretch.

There are literally hundreds of readers who have phoned, written, sent e-mails and stopped me in grocery stores and on the road during my morning runs who made me believe in myself and to them I owe an incredible gratitude for their encouragement.

And finally, I am most appreciative of LaVonne Ewing who took my computer disks and my general ideas and created a book that is the essence of what I had sought to say through out the past several years.

Jim Willard has been collecting seemingly useless facts and tantalizing tidbits of information since he was in high school. In fact, he invented a trivia board game a full two years before Trivial Pursuit got everyone sifting through their mental attic.

His office in Loveland, Colorado is literally overflowing with the 350 some dog-eared trivia books in his personal library. A horde of similarly obsessed loyal fans have made his column, "Trivially Speaking," one of the most well-read features in three Colorado newspapers. His game has been the foundation of the annual Loveland Trivia Bowl, which has been attracting trivia enthusiasts eager to match wits with the best since 1985.

Willard's whole family— three kids, four grandkids and several granddogs—has caught the trivia disease. Even his Bichon frise-Maltese pal Twoey the dog can identify 17 different kinds of dog treats.

Now that Willard is retired from 33 years at Hewlett-Packard, he's free to concentrate on his love of trivia, a fact which has his wife MJ worried. "If he keeps buying books," she smiles, "we'll have to put an addition on the house."